Adwoba Addo-Boateng

It is not just a haircut
By
Adwoba Addo-Boateng

It is not just a haircut
Adwoba Addo-Boateng

Published By Parables

All Rights Reserved. No part of this book may be reproduced or utilized in any form or by any means, electronic or mechanical, including photocopying, recording, or by any information storage and retrieval system, without permission in writing from the author.

ISBN **978-1-945698-45-3**
Printed in the United States of America

Readers should be aware that Internet Web sites offered as citations and/or sources for further information may have been changed or disappeared between the time this was written and the time it is read.

Adwoba Addo-Boateng

It is not just a haircut
By
Adwoba Addo-Boateng

ABOUT THE AUTHOR

Adwoba Addo-Boateng writes by inspiration from the Holy Spirit. She has impacted many lives through her writing ministry. She strongly believes that through Christ, we can live fulfilling lives on earth.

DEDICATION

I dedicate this book to my dear husband, Michael Kwaku Addo-Boateng. You know why ………
With lots of love and kindness
Adwoba

(Proudly Addo-Boateng)

ACKNOWLEDGEMENTS

My sincere gratitude goes to my mum and to all who supported in diverse ways, I am grateful!
Above all, to God, my all dependency, I feel so sufficient in your love.

TABLE OF CONTENTS

Chapter 1 — 7
You don't Love Your Hair Good Enough

Chapter 2 — 21
The Hired Hairdressers

Chapter 3 — 29
Salons Redefined

Chapter 4 — 55
The Craft of Hairdressing is a Gift from God

Chapter 5 — 65
Gosh! The Hairdresser Cut Off All My Hair.

Chapter 6 — 81
The Best Hairdresser is Christ

Chapter 7 — 91
Allow Him to Style Your Hair

Chapter 8 — 99
Saved with Amazing grace

INTRODUCTION

THE SEEDS

I have known Gideon for years; Gideon was a gardener who occasionally gives me seeds to plant in my backyard garden. Gideon paid me a surprise visit one day in my home and as he was leaving he gave me some seeds to plant. It was the seeds of a very sought after plant in the neighborhood that had a lot of benefits. The next day, I prepared the soil and grew the seeds. Few days after, the seeds started germinating. It grew to a point and started dying. I didn't know what was happening, so I asked my cousin who lived with me at that time whether he knew why the plants were dying. He said he didn't know why the plants were dying. I decided to watch the dying plants carefully. One day on my plant watch, I saw my cousin pouring bleach and soapy water into the soil where the plants were. I was so alarmed, I shouted from where I was standing. Hey cousin, why are you deliberately killing the plants? He looked up and said Oh, I didn't know the bleach and soapy water kills plants. Who doesn't I asked him. The killer of my plants has just been found. I told him never to put bleach and soapy water into the soil again. After a few weeks all the plants died.

Gideon came visiting again and of course to check on the plants. I told him the ordeal the plants have suffered and how they eventually died. He gave me new seeds and told me this time, watch the plants and make sure no one puts bleach and soapy water into the soil. I treated the soil and planted the seeds again, after a few weeks my garden was so green, the plants were growing so well with fresh water and natural air, and it was growing at its own pace and growing so healthy. After a few months the young plants had grown into a huge tree. I looked at the tree blossoming in my garden in awe. So I said to myself, I didn't know those seeds could grow to be this huge tree. With natural water and sunlight the seed grew to its full potential.

The problem was not with the seed or the soil but it was with the behavior of man. Man's behavior or self was getting in the way of the seed growing to its full potential. The self is one of the greatest enemies of man. By engaging in certain activities we stand in the way of God's will for us. The seed is our lives here on earth. When we allow ourselves to grow naturally in God in obedience to his word we reach our full potentials here on earth.

The seeds could be likened to our hair. God gives us great hair in all its glory but we engage in certain acts that destroys our hair completely. It is not just a haircut delves into practices of man and churches that changes our destinies here on earth and leaves us destroyed.

CHAPTER 1

YOU DON'T LOVE YOUR HAIR GOOD ENOUGH

The Big Chop

I have known Jada since my childhood days. Jada had nice curly natural hair that was admired by all. She really never paid attention to her hair but it was all healthy looking. It's been a while since I saw Jada. So one day when Jada called and said she was coming to visit I was so elated. Not only had I missed Jada but I was going to see her beautiful natural curls again.

The door bell rung and I hurriedly opened the door to see Jada. Jada had changed! She was barely unrecognizable. Her natural curly hair was replaced with fine straight hair. It suited her though but there was something about that hair that didn't seem right. Hello Jada, I said, you look good. She replied, really? I said oh yes, you look great. Jada came in and we began catching up on old times. So inquisitively, I asked Jada, what happened to your natural curly hair? Her face changed. Oh that! She quickly changed the topic to her high school heart throb that she met quite recently. And guess what he was married with six kids. Who would have thought that Brian will have as many kids as he has now?

All too soon, it was time for Jada to go. I decided to see her off to the bus station since I lived behind the bus station. Without warning a strong wind blew and we were all caught up in the moment. Jada's hair just flew away with the wind. I nearly said, Jada your hair is flying away and then I realized that that will be so rude. She was so embarrassed. I have had too many surprises today; first it was Brian with six kids then the flying hair. Oh, and then one more surprise! The true state of Jada's once lustrous curls was revealed.

Jada's hair was fragile and brittle, all her hair were thinned out possibly from the many years of chemical treatment. I felt her hair needed a remake or a redo or whatever you will call it. In this computer age we will call it a reboot. Many different hairdressers and hairstylists have worked on my friend Jada's hair possibly to make it more beautiful and possibly to keep up with the trend but have ultimately damaged the hair completely. I asked politely, have you ever thought of having a big chop? She gasped! Big chop! Did I say something very bad? Okay in case she didn't know what the big chop was. I was ready to do all the dictionary work. So I continued the big chop is when you cut off all your chemically treated hair and only the new growth of your natural hair remains.

She said to me, I don't want to cut my hair, although ever since my hair started getting damaged I wanted to. I toyed with the idea severally but I was just afraid it wouldn't grow back, she added sadly. Oh, now I know why? The fear of the unknown, why wouldn't your hair grow, I asked her? I just can't tell but I feel it will not grow, she said hesitantly. Jada, can we put your feelings away, and concentrate on what is best for your hair.

Your hair will surely grow back, it always grows back and it grows back healthy I replied. I had to psyche her for this, so I said it is better than wearing a wig, when you remove the wig you see damaged hair. Is that what you want to be seeing? Managing your natural new growth is so much easier, it is your hair. Most times a fresh start is a way to go although it might seem drastic but there is nothing to be afraid of, it is a step in getting closer to fuller beautiful hair in all its glory.

Your hair and scalp will recover from the many years effect of harsh chemicals. The hair may appear not to grow as fast as you want it but it is at a healthier pace and that is what matters. She looked at me and I smiled back. Girl, she said, there is a lot of sense in what you are saying. You are giving me the confidence to do what I have always felt like doing. Hey I was preaching here! Can I tell you something she added? Jada said; I have really missed my natural hair and I want it back. I quickly took advantage of her words and concluded that if you want something badly then you have to do all what it takes to get it.

Thumbs up for being a motivational speaker! I think I need a fresh start she added. Lo and behold the natural hair journey begun for Jada and my new role had just unfolded before me; I was an advocate for natural hair. I next saw Jada in six months and the first thing I noticed was her hair. Her hair looked so beautiful. She confided in me and said after cutting my hair I felt I had made a mistake but then again when the new growth started coming, I was so happy and if cutting my hair was a mistake then I loved that mistake but it was surely a lonely natural hair journey. We all laughed it over. She concluded; thank you so much for encouraging me to find my hair again. Points scored 100%.

So, as curious as I was, I asked Jada, why she embarked on a journey of chemically treated hair when she had such glorious hair. She said, that was the result of being a people pleaser. I wanted to make people happy at the detriment of my own life. She said she went to a new salon in her neighborhood and they convinced her with their teachings. Wow! This piece of information was intriguing. So I enquired further, what kind of salon can convince Jada to change the texture of her hair when in fact she really loved her hair.

Did they use the foot in the door technique I asked? Apparently they did, she continued it was definitely one step at a time. I was having a bad hair day and I wanted my hair to be all glorious again, as soon as I walked in I was told I was going to die. Fear gripped me so much. I didn't expect this message. Then, I was told to do daily rituals of washing my feet with wine for a week to prevent me from dying. I didn't want to die so I decided to go with the rituals, just for a period and get out, never to come back again.

Then I chipped in have you ever read Hebrews 9:13-14 that says if the blood of goats and bulls and the ashes of a heifer sprinkled on those who are ceremonially unclean sanctify them so that they are outwardly clean. **How much more, then, will the blood of Christ, who through the eternal Spirit offered himself**

unblemished to God, cleanse our consciences from acts that lead to death, so that we may serve the living God! How would I have known that, I hardly read the bible? It was so costly as well; she continued I had to buy a new bottle of wine every day. I chipped in again, haven't you heard that Jesus saves for free, all what you have to do is to believe in him.

Hmm, it was like I was not thinking: I totally forgot about this information, before I realized, I had turned into something else. I had adjusted so well that I was so comfortable with their way of doing things. I began hating others because everyone was a prime suspect in my predicament. I was fighting battles I was not supposed to be fighting, I had to interrupt so I did, what about Ephesians 6:12 that says **for we wrestle not against flesh and blood, but against principalities, against powers, against the rulers of the darkness of this world, against spiritual wickedness in high places.**

Did I ever think of that, I was too involved in the neck of things that when I go to functions I will not eat because I was so scared of eating food not cooked by myself. I was living as an island. Fear ruled me, it was so terrible, and I was told demons could be passed on from dresses to dresses. I couldn't visit my favorite thrift shop anymore, my cousin's designer hand me downs was no more accepted, let alone worn by me. I was told Christianity makes you rich so if you were not getting rich then you were not sowing high financial seeds enough. I had to interrupt, I was getting angry , **If only for this life we have hope in Christ, we are of all people most to be pitied (1 Corinthians 15:19).**

Jada continued, sometimes the hair dresser will secretly call me aside when there was an impending harvest and ask me to sow huge financial seeds. He said that was the only way I could be blessed. She added; one day, I had just received my bonus from working so hard at work, I wanted to surprise my mom with a gift but I decided to go to the salon first. I was told to give away 5000 dollars to break a generational curse. Wait! I interrupted, even in the old testament in Ezekiel 18:1-3 the word of the LORD came to me: "What do you people mean by quoting this proverb about the land of Israel:"

**'The parents eat sour grapes,
and the children's teeth are set on edge'? "**

As surely as I live, declares the Sovereign LORD, you will no longer quote this proverb in Israel. For everyone belongs to me, the parent as well as the child—both alike belong to me. The one who sins is the one who will die.

Even Jesus Christ came with a superior covenant and ministry, the ministry of grace and truth. In him we are saved if we believe in him. I didn't know this, she added. In fact, there was always something. In a confused look, I asked why you didn't leave. I left to another salon and it was so bad there too, the abuse was terrible and they tell you that if you leave you won't survive anywhere. That is real abuse! I said, they call it loyalty, she added.

The prayers were more like manual labor. We had to clap our hands whilst praying and they said the harder you clap, the more demons die. We prayed till we were weary yet no positive results and even with no peace. It was if we were pushing God away with our prayers. I asked Jada, Does the prayer flow from your heart. No, it was all about the clapping. Jada opened her palms revealing blisters in her palms. Now, I was feeling so sorry for Jada. Oh No, I exclaimed; Prayer is the outpouring of your heart to your maker that is all and a true prayer to God comes with so much peace. Even in the Apostle Paul's letter to the Philippians, he said when we pray; the peace that transcends our understanding is given to us and that peace will guard our hearts and minds in Christ Jesus. Wow! You must have gone through a lot. Understatement! She readily said. The good news is that, when I last came here, I had one foot out but I needed that necessary push and thank God you encouraged me to cut all my chemically treated hair off and grow my natural hair.

Before I came here, I looked at myself in the mirror one morning and I obviously didn't like what I saw. My hair was awful and I hated it. I had also gained a lot of weight that my thighs were rubbing against each other, I couldn't walk properly. I didn't like what I had become. Let me walk you through the situation at that time. I was full of the flesh that I had gained weight in inappropriate places and I was so unhappy. I grew so bitter that I was always fighting battles I wasn't supposed to be fighting.

What was I supposed to do to lose the weight and walk properly again so that I can stop being a heavy weight fighter. I decided to write a to-do list but I just could not conform to that list. I had a lot on my mind and external pressures were settling in. No matter how hard I tried, things were permanently on fire and I gained more weight and I fought more battles. Also one secret was that I was afraid of appearing weak to people around me, so I appeared strong in all areas even though I was suffering deep inside me. Truth be told, I was suffering in all aspects of my life. My hair was the suffering the most, because it was the first thing people saw and everyone realized I had issues.

So I decided to find change, where was change? I looked and looked for change but it amounted to nothing. Now, I was getting frustrated. In my frustration and depression when all things looked so stagnant in life I found the most beautiful change ever. The day you urged me to cut my chemically treated hair, was the day I found change. I found Christ!

Immediately, I found Christ I lost a significant amount of weight. Christ gave me the perfect weight trainer that was Mr. Holy Spirit that helped me in my weight loss journey by turning me away from things of the flesh. The acts of the flesh are obvious: sexual immorality, impurity and debauchery; idolatry and witchcraft; hatred, discord, jealousy, fits of rage, selfish ambition, dissensions, factions and envy; drunkenness, orgies, and the like. I warn you, as I did before, that those who live like this will not inherit the kingdom of God (Galatians 5:19-21).

Mr. Holy Spirit was with me all the time and he charges no fee. When I felt like engaging in the things I used to do in the past he was there to prompt me. He was such a great helper. **But the Advocate, the Holy Spirit, whom the Father will send in my name, will teach you all things and will remind you of everything I have said to you (John 14:26).**

I seriously had to unleash all those teachings, read the bible myself and submit to the guidance of the Holy Spirit. I travelled that lonely path and I am glad I found that path. On why I wore the wig, my hair was damaged beyond repairs so I had to borrow someone's hair. We all burst into laughter. It was funny, but it was serious!

All my fears went away because the love I was being given was perfect. There is no fear in love. But perfect love drives out fear, because fear has to do with punishment. The one who fears is not made perfect in love. (1 John 4:18). I was now been led by the Spirit and I had become a favorite child of God that I never want that spot taken.

What about my weakness, did my weakness go away? My weakness didn't go away but His strength was made perfect in my weakness so that Christ's power will rest on me. I was now living by the grace and stopped fighting battles I was not supposed to fight for we wrestle not against flesh and blood, but against principalities, against powers, against the rulers of the darkness of this world, against spiritual wickedness in high places (Ephesians 6:12).

And now to my favorite part, my thighs were not rubbing against each other anymore. I couldn't only walk well I could even run. Therefore, since we are surrounded by such a great cloud of witnesses, let us throw off everything that hinders and the sin that so easily entangles. And let us run with perseverance the race marked out for us, fixing our eyes on Jesus, the pioneer and perfecter of faith. For the joy set before him he endured the cross, scorning its shame, and sat down at the right hand of the throne of God (Hebrews 12: 1-2).

There were and are certainly challenges but in spite of the challenges he gives me peace that cannot be understood by human minds. I am at a happier place today and I look into the mirror today and smile that I can do all things through Christ who strengthens me.

Jada, you remind me so much of my natural hair journey. You also went through this she asked? Of course, and so my narration begun.

My Natural Hair Journey

I had attended many churches and I was blown here and there by many teachings, rituals and practices. I was getting nowhere; I didn't feel like myself, I seriously felt that something was missing. Church going has become so ritualistic for me. I don't even know what I had turned into. The teachings were not helping me; my bible was always dusty because I never read it. I had no time. I was always rushing in to catch my favorite spot to a church program. I would say, I had become so addicted to these church programs!

My hair was damaged; I wanted my true self back so I embarked on my natural hair journey. Mine was so catastrophic, because I really had long locks. I cut all my chemically treated hair within minutes, I wanted out, I wanted my own hair. I began reading and living the bible, I realized I was changing; I was evolving into who I was when God created me. I began loving no matter what although there were many challenges but the good Lord helped me through. Eureka! My hair started growing healthier and beautiful in ways I never thought off. Everyone was admiring my hair everywhere I went. I felt so happy. This was the kind of life I wanted all along.

When we attend some churches (salons) we treat our hair with chemicals and the texture of the hair changes. We realize that our hair has lost its natural texture and then we want to revert to our natural hair or what we were actually meant to be. The best way is to do the big chop which will liberate you from all the practices and rituals of (salons/churches) and start your natural hair journey with Christ. But do not forget dear friends: with the lord a day is like a 1000 years and a 1000 years is like a day (2 Peter 3:8**). God will restore the many years that you wasted before surrendering your life to Jesus.** And I will restore to you the years that the locust has eaten, the cankerworm and the caterpillar and the palmerworm, my great army which I sent among you (Joel 2:25). Even in the days of restoration, everyday won't be an amazing hair day there may be trials, tests and temptations but no temptation will overtake you except what is common to mankind. And God is faithful he will not let you be tempted beyond what you can bear. But when you are tempted, he will also provide a way out so that you can endure it (1 Corinthians 10:13). After doing the big chop you learn new things, you put off your old self and you hear the Holy Spirit and submit to his guidance. You learn to be content and you begin to love the rich density of your hair. And oh! The benefits of the big chop: it is less costly, it saves time and energy, and it gives you so much relief that you are all natural. The confidence and the swag and the freedom it gives you are beyond what you will ever think.

Caring For Your New Growth

Cutting of split ends (pruning)

Christ is the trimmer that will cut all split ends so that the hair can grow more beautifully. (John 15:1), I am the true vine and my father is the vinedresser. Every branch in me that does not bear fruit He takes away; and every branch that bears fruit he prunes, that it may bear more fruit.

Building Your Faith and Trust in God

I know every Christian hates the pruning process in fact even the plants hate it. Pruning (split ends trimming) is done by Christ to make the person more fruitful by cutting unwanted / damaged parts of the tree or hair so that it can grow well in all its glory. There was a time in my life that nothing was working. I prayed to God to help me with the situation but it looked as if God was silent. I asked God severally why he was not answering me and all what I was getting was suffering to more suffering. It was so hard! It was like everyone has left you. My only friend was Jesus! And he has become my rock that all other grounds were sinking sand. I realized that nobody could help me, if God didn't so I had to rely on God for everything. As painful as it was I came to a new definition of faith: "everything that the Lord does is good" and I began to develop immense trust in the Lord. I had grown up in a way that I only trusted God when things were going as I have planned it and when it is going the other way round, I feel it isn't God. I passed through the suffering with the word of God. Of course some days were that bad I couldn't even read the word of God. It helped me develop certain attitudes that were missing in my life prior to finding God. I learnt long suffering, tolerance, endurance, patience and resilience, the Gardener was at its work, or the split ends were being trimmed so that my hair will look more beautiful. When a hair is being cut no matter how small it is being cut, it experiences some shock and I am sure no hair likes that shock. But when the hair begins to grow, It grows more beautifully and healthier and you even have the peace that cannot be understood by human minds. **I began to trust God even though it didn't make sense.**

Revitalizing Love Shampoo

The main ingredient in the revitalizing shampoo is Love. Christ is love. For your hair to grow more beautifully and healthy we need to imitate Christ by loving others as ourselves. Love covers a multitude of sins. When you love irrespective of whatever you have been through and however you have been treated you walk in the light. And your light shines so brightly that it begins to affect other people around you. People see your hair in all its glory and want to have that type of hair. "You are the light of the world. A town built on a hill cannot be hidden. Neither do people light a lamp and put it under a bowl. Instead they put it on its stand, and it gives light to everyone in the house. (Matthew 5:14-15)

Hair Spray

Aroma of Christ (Ephesians 5:2)

Follow God's example, therefore as dearly loved children and walk in the way of love just as Christ loved us and gave himself up for us a fragrant offering and sacrifice to God. When we imitate Christ in all our doings we always radiate a sweet fragrance because we have the favor of God which follows us everywhere we go.

Avoiding Excessive Heat (Galatians 5)

Live according to the spirit not according to the flesh for the act of the flesh kills. Walk in the spirit and you shall not fulfill the lust of the flesh. For the flesh lusts against the spirit and the spirit against the flesh and these are in contrary to one another. By avoiding excessive heat so that it doesn't damage the hair, we do away with acts of the flesh such us adultery, fornication, uncleanness, lewdness, idolatry, sorcery, hatred, contentions jealousies, outbursts of wrath, selfish ambition, dissensions, heresies, envy, murders, drunkenness, revelries and the like.

Your goal is to remain in Christ and being in Christ is continual, whether you are happy or sad, high or low. Who shall separate us from the love of Christ? Shall trouble or hardship or persecution or famine or nakedness or danger or sword? (Romans 8:35)

Redefining Your Breakthrough

The focus is not about miracles or financial breakthroughs, but the focus should be craving a deeper intimacy with God for his will to be done. Many of us want more from God instead of wanting more of God, so instead of trying to know God we rather seek miracles and it ends so badly. This explains why most people go to church and they get disappointed all the time because they are seeking more of material things. But when we rather seek first the kingdom of God and his righteousness, all other things are added to it. In so doing, we allow Christ to come into our hearts and change the heart which is the greatest miracle. Then we journey with him and everyday becomes a new experience with him. So that he can continue molding our hearts to be whatever he wants it to be.

Why People Visit Salons?

Many people go to church for various reasons, I once run a poll and asked people reasons why they go to church. The answers I received were to have fellowship with God, to hear the message of God, to grow in the knowledge of God, to build their faith and trust in God, to belong to a group where they will be loved, to pray, to receive God's blessings and miracles, to find God, to worship God, to find solutions to problems, to get support, to make friends, to feed their soul with the word of God and amongst others. People go to church with all these expectations and hopes but most come back home disappointed with unmet goals.

Metaphorically, people go to churches to grow their hair however most come back with an unsolicited haircut that makes them unrecognizable. The big question is why is it so? A church should be a safety net where a group of people gather in accordance with their faith to build themselves up in the Lord. A church can be likened to a salon, where people from all walks of life troop in to get their hair done and to improve upon their appearance. People (Church members) walk in with various needs and their needs are supposed to be met by these hairdressers (Pastors/Leads).

When people go to the salon, their hair gets nourished with hair food. When the hair is thinning out, the hair is trimmed to help it grow back beautifully and stronger. When the hair is knotted and cannot be combed through, a "detangler" is used to make combing easier. When the hair is dirty, the hair is washed with shampoo and conditioned to make styling easier. All these efforts are in an attempt to make the hair grow and look beautiful. That is how a pastor or lead is supposed to act to shape our lives through admonishing us with the word of God, giving godly counseling to members where need be and the members are encouraged in their faith. In sum, we go to church to grow our hair and look beautiful in all glory and we end up with destroyed hair that distorts our image, cripples us financially, destroys our relationships with families and friends and worst of all it destroys our lives completely."

Can We Find and Grow Our Natural Hair in Salons?

It depends on the teaching that is given. If the teachings are on Christ, you are at a good place. Christ is love. Any teaching that goes contrary to Christ's teaching is something you should beware off. Test every spirit and hold on to what is good, any teaching that doesn't acknowledge that Jesus Christ is Lord and has come in the flesh is anti -Christ.

Testing Every Spirit

A lady had a problem with the husband; the husband wanted a divorce because the wife was not submissive and very disrespectful to him. The lead called the lady to sow a specific amount of money and he made the lady mention the husband's name seven times. The lady came back with good news that the husband has decided not to divorce her. I found it very strange, there is no such thing in the word of God.

The lady has to allow Christ to come into her life, and then her attitude towards her husband will change. Then they will be heirs together in the grace of life. Are we looking for temporary quick fixes or we are looking for a permanent change in our lives led by Christ. Dear friends, do not believe every spirit, but test the spirits to see whether they are from God, because many false prophets have gone out into the world.(1 John 4:1)

We should all come to the knowledge, faith and unity of the son of God so that we can experience the fullness of Christ, so that we will no longer be blown about by every wind of teaching and by the cunning and craftiness of people in their deceitful scheming (Ephesians 4)

Adwoba Addo-Boateng

CHAPTER 2

THE HIRED HAIRDRESSERS

Take a Selfie

Before we enter a church, we should take a very good look at ourselves; perhaps we should take a selfie. God created us uniquely; accordingly we are fearfully and wonderfully made (Psalm 139:14). We are all on earth for a particular purpose, to find that path that will lead us to whom we were born to be and that purpose of life can be actually achieved through Christ. *Thomas said to him, Lord, we don't know where you are going, so how can we know the way?" Jesus answered, "I am the way and the truth and the life. No one comes to the Father except through me*. (John 14:5-6).

The word of God is the way; we are supposed to live according to the teachings of Christ, so that you will be able to find your true purpose in life. James 1:22-25 cautions us that" *Do not merely listen to the word, and so deceive yourselves. Do what it says. Anyone who listens to the word but does not do what it says is like someone who looks at his face in a mirror and after looking at himself, goes away and immediately forgets what he looks like. But the man who looks intently into the perfect law that gives freedom, and continues to do this, not forgetting what he has heard, but doing it- he will be blessed in what he does"*.

A man I knew way back was a servant of God. Accordingly, he used his gift freely to preach the gospel. He was loved by all his church members and all who came into contact with him. He visited another church one day and he was told many things by the lead there. The lead there then asked him to join his church or else he may lose his life since he was battling with some illnesses. The lead claimed he was the messiah and he was the only one who could save him. This servant of God left his church and joined this new church all in the name of being saved from death. I found it very unusual, how was he convinced to leave his church and join another church for supposed healing. When it was only God who saves and God is omnipresent, he is everywhere; all we have to do is to believe in him. Eventually, the man died exactly two weeks after he joined this new church. Then I remembered that we were cautioned in the bible in Matthew 23:23-24 *"At that time if anyone says to you, 'Look, here is the Messiah!' or, 'There he is!' do not believe it. For false messiahs and false prophets will appear and perform great signs and wonders to deceive, if possible, even the elect. See, I have told you ahead of time"*.

Today Leads

In the temple in those days, people were using the temple as a market place, which is certainly no different from what is happening these days.

Churches are springing up in every corner; you can easily locate one in your neighborhood so commuting to church is not a barrier to attending church these days. However, some leads have diverted from preaching the true gospel to merchandising the gospel. I once went to church and I thought I had entered a mall. Everything was for sale from water to anointing oils; it was such a sight to behold. Some have cleverly made a shop outside the church to make money from these innocent ones who want to seek the face of God. *Matthew 21:12-13 Jesus entered the temple area and drove out all who were buying and selling there. He overturned the tables of the money changers and the benches of those selling doves. It is written, my house will be called, a house of prayer, but you are making it a den of robbers"*

The Hired Hands

Matthew 9: 37-38 *"Then he said to his disciples, the harvest is plentiful but the workers are few. Ask the Lord of the harvest, therefore to send out workers into his harvest field".* A staunch member of a church was praying in a meeting house in front of other members of a group. When she started sweating profusely whilst praying, immediately, the lady collapsed and the first thing the group did was to call the lead instead of calling upon God. The group called and called the lead but the lead never picked the call. The whole group ended up at the church premises where they thought they will find the lead but the lead was nowhere to be found. The group then decided to wait at the Church premises with the dying lady with hopes that the lead will arrive to pray for the lady and heal her. They waited and waited, called all his phones but to no avail. Eventually, when there was no sign of the lead and from all possible indications the woman was dying, the group then decided to take the lady to the hospital for possible treatment.

When they got to the hospital, the lady was pronounced dead on arrival. Calling on the name of God not man is a right and privilege for all of us, whenever and for whatever reason. He is our father and he is ever ready to listen to us. One cannot therefore blame the group because their minds have been brainwashed that the lead is the only one who can save hence their behavior.

In another event in another church, there was a story of a lady who was diagnosed with fibroid, her doctor asked her to get prepared for a surgical removal of the fibroid. The lady went to church one day when the lead asked her not to remove the fibroid and that through prayers he will heal her. The lady obliged, and the fibroid generated into other complications and she lost her life eventually.

The real healer is God and he heals through many ways including medicine. **Oh, the depth of the riches and the wisdom and knowledge of God! How unsearchable his judgments, and his paths beyond tracing out. (Romans 11:33)**. All what we have to do is to trust him through the process and commune with him continuously to know his perfect will for us. We are all hired hands and the real shepherd is Jesus. However *the hired hand is not the Shepherd who owns the sheep. So when he sees the wolf coming, he abandons the sheep and runs away. Then the wolf attacks the flock and scatters it. The man runs away because he is a hired hand and cares nothing for the sheep (John 10: 12-13).*

Comic Leading

"From the days of John the Baptist until now, the kingdom of heaven has been subjected to violence, and the violent people have been raiding it" (Matthew 11:12)

I was moving to a new house, hence I needed help with packing my belongings for the moving van to take to the new house, so I called on my neighbor to help me with the packing, we had hardly finished when the moving van entered my yard with a loud screeching noise resulting from the depleted brake pads. There was loud music playing in the car with three young men nodding to the beat of the music. They sluggishly got down and asked which boxes were going. In the course of moving the boxes into the van, they were talking about leads, it drew my attention and I engaged in the conversation.

A popular figure had died in the country and the young men were of the view that the leads should have saved him. I found it very strange, when have leads been given the power to save on their own; **it is only God who saves**! We are saved only through Christ. They argued and argued and came to the conclusion that the leads have the power to do everything including making or unmaking you. Wow! I exclaimed! My intention to talk them out of it proved futile because they were so strong in their beliefs. I sat down quietly thinking about the whole situation. It really was a bugger!

One other day, my nanny and I were engaged in a conversation about leads. Where do you go to church I asked? A church that kills all enemies through prayers she replied. Then I further asked why do you pray to kill people? She said, her lead asked them to do it and that if we do not kill the "Goliaths" we will not succeed in life. In Paul's letter to the Galatians, he warned the Galatians to desist from such practices *which is really no gospel at all. Evidently some people are throwing you into confusion and are trying to pervert the gospel of Christ. (Galatians 1:7).* This information was so new to me; I had never heard of such a thing, is our God not greater than all powers? *In him was life, and that life was the light of all mankind. The light shines in the darkness, and the darkness has not overcome it (John 1:4-5).* If the darkness itself cannot comprehend the light, why think of the darkness when you are in Christ, and you have the light. ***When Jesus spoke again to the people, he said, "I am the light of the world. Whoever follows me will never walk in darkness, but will have the light of life" (John 8:12).*** So why do you have to kill someone in order to be successful in life? Ephesians 6:12 says *"for our struggle is not against flesh and blood, but against the rulers, against the authorities, against the powers of this dark world and against the spiritual forces of evil in the heavenly realms".* In addition, Jesus also said *"But I tell you, love your enemies and pray for those who persecute you". (Matthew 5:44).* Loving your enemies and praying for them no matter what was an instruction Jesus gave. ***Therefore confess your sins to each other and pray for each other so that you may be healed. The prayer of a righteous person is powerful and effective (James 5:16)***

Moreover, the story of David and Goliath in the bible is a story that shows the strength of God in spite of our weaknesses. God is made perfect in our weaknesses. When we are weak, then he is strong. When we exhibit the contrite heart and give all power to him to make us into whatever he chooses, he comes through for us.

When Moses was sent to Pharaoh by God, he communicated his weakness to God by telling him, he is not eloquent, but God assured him that his strength will be made perfect in his weakness.

In Luke chapter 15, Jesus told the story of the prodigal son. In summary, there were two brothers who lived with their father. The younger one told his father to **give** him the share of the estate and went into the world whilst the older son stayed with his father. The younger one spent everything he had and became poor. He came to his senses and realized that he has a father who loved him and he was even willing to be a hired hand in his father's house due to the fact that he knew that the hired men were treated better in his father's house. ***Better is one day in your courts than a thousand elsewhere; I would rather be a doorkeeper in the house of my God than dwell in the tents of the wicked. (Psalm 84:10).***

When he came to repentance, he told his father in verse 19. "I am no longer worthy to be called your son, **make** me like one of your hired men". The young son wanted to live his life his way in the beginning. When he realized he had taken an unproductive route, he was willing to take a U-turn and abide in the vine so that he will be fruitful. ***Remain in me, as I also remain in you. No branch can bear fruit by itself; it must remain in the vine. Neither can you bear fruit unless you remain in me. (John 15:4).*** The young son allowed God to make him to be whatever he wanted him to be. He was humble enough to put God in charge of his life. He was willing to be clay in the hands of the Potter for God to mold him into whatever he desired. God did exceedingly and abundantly above all that he thought off or even imagined. When he came to repentance, the grace was fully activated in his life and he was accepted back as a son.

"In the last times there will be scoffers who will follow their own ungodly desires." These are the people who divide you, who follow mere natural instincts and do not have the Spirit. But you, dear friends, by building yourselves up in your most holy faith and praying in the Holy Spirit, keep yourselves in God's love as you wait for the mercy of our Lord Jesus Christ to bring you to eternal life. (Jude 1)

Rationale Underlying Behavior

Matthew 15:8-9 "these people honor me with their lips, but their hearts are far away from me. They worship me in vain; their teachings are but rules taught by men".

In my level 300 psychology class, I sat at the corner in one of the Lecture rooms when suddenly the Lecturer budged in with a smiling face. It was a social psychology class. Then she said today is going to be exciting. The students started murmuring amongst themselves. What was she going to talk about? My interest heightened because one of my best subjects was social psychology. I suddenly sat up when she mentioned Jim Jones. I had heard that name before. So I became more attentive as she narrated the story of James Warren Jones. James Warren Jones was an American religious leader, who initiated and was responsible for a mass suicide and mass murder in Jonestown Guyana. He believed communism was the correct social order in compliance with God's will.

Detailing further, Jim jones was a leader of Peoples Temple Cult who led his members to suicide by drinking poison. I kept pondering over this story. How could he have achieved that, driving people to commit suicide? He had brainwashed their minds for them to agree with anything he will say. Their actions were dependent on the minds of their leader. What of their own minds? People had changed their own attitudes in order to identify with the group.

One girl shared her story of how she escaped three weeks earlier because she felt it wasn't right and her freedom was being held captive. Why do people feel less important when a leader with perceived power restricts them?

The Stanford Prison Experiment (1971) was an experiment that investigated the psychological effects of perceived power between people in authority that is prison guards and people whose freedom have been taken away from them that is prisoners. This experiment was led by Philip Zimbardo, a psychology professor using college students. The study was conducted to show the extent that the power of rules, roles and group identity makes ordinary people behave in a certain manner. In sum, people's individuality was taken away and was ruled by fear by people in supposed authority.

The study concluded that the fake prison situation rather than an individual's characteristics caused a participants behavior. The prisoners begun to accept their roles as subjects to the prison guards owing to the fact that the prison guards were highest in authority and they had control over them. The Stanford Prison Experiment showed a positive relationship between power and social roles and external pressures that influence our behavior.

What is a church? The word church is derived from the Greek word "ekklesia" which means assembly or called out ones. A

Church is also the gathering of people who believe in the body of Christ that is believers.

In these modern days, some cults are operating like churches and they have spread like wild fire. There is a leader with perceived power who manipulates the members for his own selfish gain. Members freedom are taken away and they are supposed to be under the dictates of the leader which is detrimental to their well - being. These leaders make decisions for their members as to how they should live their lives. The members also out of fear subject themselves to this person with perceived power and eventually their behavior changes in order to conform to a group. They normally say "everyone is doing it", why should I be different? They want to be loved and acknowledged by the leader and gradually the leader becomes the focus and not Christ.

Christianity is love; *there is no fear in love. But perfect love drives out fear, because fear has to do with punishment. The one who fears is not made perfect in love. (1 John 4:18).*

A Church that I went to will call people in front of the congregation to give money for supposed financial blessings. I was not a fan of that initially but when I started going to that church, I conformed totally because I wanted to have an identity to the group. The more someone gave money, the more the leader liked him or her. In effect, everyone wanted to be in the leader's good books therefore they gave out money not because they wanted to give to the Lord but for the mere fact that they will be loved and cherished by their leader. In short, the fear of being hated by the leader was the motivation factor for conforming.

In Exodus 3:7, The Lord said, 'I have indeed seen the misery of my people in Egypt. I have heard them crying out because of their slave drivers and I am concerned about their suffering. In verse 8, he made mention of the fact that it is only he that can rescue the Israelites out of their sorrows. The same way, Christ is the only lead who can save or rescue us out of our sorrows.

CHAPTER 3
SALONS REDEFINED

The Church Is a Unified Body for Unifying Purposes

The church is one body made up of different parts. God has appointed apostles, prophets, teachers, and workers of miracles, those having gifts of healing, helpers, administrators and tongue speakers. All these gifts are coordinated with love. The Apostle Paul then described what love is in 1st Corinthians 13:4 *"Love is patient, love is kind. It does not envy, it does not boast, it is not proud. It does not dishonor others, it is not self-seeking, it is not easily angered, and it keeps no record of wrongs. Love does not delight in evil but rejoices with the truth. It always protects, always trusts, always hopes, and always perseveres. Love never fails. But where there are prophecies, they will cease; where there are tongues, they will be stilled; where there is knowledge, it will pass away".*

The Real Function of a Church

In Acts 4:32 the real function of the church is brought to light. "All the believers were one in heart and mind. No one claimed that any of their possessions was their own, but they shared everything they had. With great power the apostles continued to testify to the resurrection of the Lord Jesus. And God's grace was so powerfully at work in them all that there were no needy persons among them. For time to time those who owned land or houses sold them, brought the money from the sales and put it at the apostle's feet, and it was **distributed to anyone who had need.**"

The Church According To Acts of the Apostles

Fellowship of the believers
1. They devoted themselves to the Apostles teaching and fellowship and the breaking of bread and prayer.
2. They believers had everything in common because they sold their possessions and distributed to those in need.
3. They shared food with others in their homes which they ate together with glad and sincere hearts.
4. They praised God all the time
5. The Apostles healed in Jesus' name
6. The people were being saved owing to the message of repentance being preached by the Apostles and God added to their numbers.
7. The Apostles were filled with the Holy Spirit and spoke the word of God boldly.
8. They faced persecution, but relied on God through it all to preach the good news that Jesus is the Messiah.

We are all Intercessors

We are all supposed to pray for people according to the spirit and the will of God. In Acts 12:5, the church earnestly prayed for Peter's release and God's will was done. In addition, being an intercessor is emphasized in James 5:16 that we need to confess our sins to each other and pray for each other so that we may be healed. It concludes that the prayer of righteous person is powerful and effective.

Furthermore, in the Apostle Paul's letter to the Thessalonians, he prays (intercedes) for all believers that God may make us worthy of his calling, and that by his power he may bring to fruition every desire for goodness and every deed prompted by faith. Accordingly, in the Apostle Paul's letter to the Ephesians, he made mention of the fact that he had never stopped praying for the entire Lord's people.

He also petitioned God for them that God may give them the spirit of wisdom and revelation, so that they may know him better.

Serving God in Truth in Churches

During the days of the early church, the Christians out of their own desire sold their possessions and distributed it to everyone in need. However, there was a man called Ananias who sold his possession and brought part of the money and laid it at the apostle's feet with his wife's Sapphira's full knowledge. Now, Peter asked him why he has kept part of the money he received from the sale of the possession. Peter continued that he has not lied to men but to God. He fell down and died His wife Sapphira also came in and lied about the price of the sale of the possession, she also fell down and died and fear gripped the church. Remember that God is not mocked **"Do not be deceived: God cannot be mocked. A man reaps what he sows. (Galatians 6:7).** There was no obligation at that time to be compelled to do things. Everyone was entitled to his or her freedom, for where the spirit of God is, there is freedom. Doing things wholeheartedly for God is what matters. For the Lord does not look at the things man looks at. Man looks at the outward appearance, but the Lord looks at the heart. (1 Samuel 6:7).

Our actions are like seeds, whatever seed you plant, you will reap whatever you sow, for instance if you sow a bad seed, you will surely reap bad fruits but when you sow good seeds by abiding in the vine, you will definitely reap good fruits. A good tree is recognized by its fruit.

A church is supposed to serve as a safety net for people where even the poor and the dejected are loved, encouraged, uplifted, motivated, taught and built up in Christ and of course seeking the welfare of the people and helping people to know the grace that Christ has in store for them if they believe.

Churches (Salons) Today

What do we see today? The Church has been turned into a den of thieves and creating high levels of income inequality and members are ruled with fear. The poor are getting poorer and the rich are getting richer all in the name of sowing seeds to get miracles at the end of it all, members are greatly oppressed.

Some Churches are plagued by arrogant, boastful and manipulative individuals and unfortunately these people serve as leaders of the Church which is very comical. **Do not love the world or anything in the world. If anyone loves the world, love for the Father is not in them. For everything in the world—the lust of the flesh, the lust of the eyes, and the pride of life—comes not from the Father but from the world. The world and its desires pass away, but whoever does the will of God lives forever (1 John 2:15-17).**

What baffles me is that most of these leads engaging in such acts are actually called by God but got caught up in the frenzy of quick success especially when they look at their peers possessing huge buildings and driving very expensive cars. There is nothing bad if one possesses these things, it becomes bad when one confidently tricks members to acquire these things.

Characteristics of Bad Salons

> - Cults distort the gospel of Christ, by misinterpreting the bible for their own selfish gain. What is the true gospel of Christ? The true gospel of Christ is love. God created us in his own image and God is love, so our primary purpose on earth is to love. Love does not include deception. Love is truth. 2 Corinthians 4: 2, cautions us not to use deception or distort the word of God. On the contrary, we should preach the truth plainly. Paul the Apostle wrote to the Galatians in chapter 1:8-9 emphasizing the fact that only the true gospel should be preached. He added that even if ministers or angels should preach any other gospel let them be eternally condemned. *Leads are supposed to preach the gospel, not with wisdom and eloquence, lest the cross of Christ be emptied of its power* (1 Corinthians 1:17)

➢ Members tend to rely on the lead for all spiritual knowledge and interpersonal relationship with God is downplayed or is nonexistent.

➢ The leader is autocratic and does not allow any divergent view from other members of the group. In so doing he turns to manipulate his followers with his own ideas and knowledge. *Now the Lord is the Spirit, and where the Spirit of the Lord is, there is freedom.* 2 Corinthians 3:17. Permission must be sought from the leader before a certain decision is made in order to be saved but Ephesians 2:8-9 says ; *For it is by grace you have been saved, through faith—and this is not from yourselves, it is the gift of God not by works, so that no one can boast. For we are God's handiwork, created in Christ Jesus to do good works, which God prepared in advance for us to do.*

➢ Members trust is in the Charismatic Leader but not in the Lord.

"Cursed is the one who trusts in man,
  who draws strength from mere flesh
  and whose heart turns away from the LORD.
That person will be like a bush in the wastelands;
  they will not see prosperity when it comes.
They will dwell in the parched places of the desert,
  in a salt land where no one lives. (Jeremiah)

Bad Practices of Some Churches/Salons

1. Brain Washing

Most leads start erasing your mind of any knowledge you might have acquired and engage you deeply in the neck of things you would never want to normally engage in. Then you suddenly rely on him and make him your all in all and subconsciously you automatically feel your salvation is in his hand.

2. Consulting mediums/ Spiritists

A church was having its annual "miracle" program and every member was made to sow a seed of a certain amount to avert a supposed death of a member. The church members quickly gave out that amount of money as seeds to secure their lives. A pregnant church member sadly died two weeks later after child birth. So in effect, what did that money do? No money can save a soul; it is only Christ who saves. Then the lead came out with a flimsy excuse as to why the lady died. He said, he called the spirit of the dead girl and asked her why she died. He then asked the girl whether he gave that money out as a seed. According to him, the girl said no. So to him the girl died because she did not give that amount of money out as a seed to avert her own death. Please note that no money can buy grace. It is by grace we are saved. And by the way what is a Christian doing with the spirit of the dead?

When men tell you to consult mediums and spiritists, who whisper and mutter, should not a people inquire of their God? Why consult the dead on behalf of the living? If they do not speak according to this word, they have no light of dawn. (Isaiah 8:19-20).

3. Members are given prosthetic legs

Unfortunately, in this era in Churches, people's faith has been replaced by a Lead's faith. Our faith has been put into the dust bin and fear and anxiety has taken over our lives. Isaiah 52:7 reads:

How beautiful on the mountains
   are the feet of those who bring good news,
who proclaim peace,
   who bring good tidings,
   who proclaim salvation,
who say to Zion,
   "Your God reigns!"

Your whole body is supported by the legs. The legs support movement and it takes the body anywhere it wants to go. When one's legs are cut off, he or she cannot move unless he or she is given prosthetic legs. The prosthetic leg no matter how well it is made cannot be equated to a natural leg. Even though you can now move, your movements are somewhat restricted and there are a lot of things you cannot do. You definitely cannot run a good race comparatively. When you rely on comic leads for all your needs, these leads cut off your natural legs and replace it with prosthetic legs. Your faith in Christ becomes impaired; you therefore cannot build your faith and trust in God. Faith is a gift from God it is not attained by compulsion. The Apostle Paul talked of running a good race that is having faith in God. *"I have fought the good fight, I have finished the race, I have kept the faith. Now there is in store for me the crown of righteousness, which the Lord, the righteous Judge, will award to me on that day—and not only to me, but also to all who have longed for his appearing"*. (2 Timothy 4:7-8). So if your natural legs has been cut off and has been replaced with prosthetic legs, then your walk with God is shaky. Go the natural way in serving God just listen to the still small voice when all other things are quiet.

4. Blessing Exchange

Most times, the blessings that God has given you are far greater than what these leads make you pray for. Before he formed you, he knew you; before you were born he set you apart. All that is required of us to do is to believe in the one that he sent (John 6:29). In John 15, Jesus gave the instruction that in order to be fruitful we need to remain in the vine. Remaining in Christ means to take all your needs from him. When a branch is in the vine, the branch takes all its nutrients from the vine in order to grow. If the branch detaches itself from the vine, it will not grow well and it will eventually die.

5. Engaging in Manual Work

The Lord's Prayer is a sample prayer taught by Christ. The overall content of that prayer is to pray under God's reign that is putting God on the throne for his purpose in our lives to be fulfilled. He asked us to just ask for our daily bread and not asking to achieve our bucket list in life. It is good to pray for the things we want to achieve but at the end of it all, let us pray according to his will (1 John 5). For when we pray according to his will, he hears us.

A man called John wanted a position in government at all cost. Someone connected him to a politician who could work things out for him. He tried to see this man, but somehow he could not see him due to circumstances beyond him. The man had various excuses, he was always running late. After many fruitless efforts, he gave up. He then decided to put God in charge of getting that position. A year later, someone called from the office of the president with that same job offer. How his curriculum vitae got there remains a mystery till date. When God was in charge, he had the job through grace and not efforts when he was ready for the job.

6. Running Recruitment Agencies

I have been to some churches, where the lead will command the church members to go and win souls for Christ so that they would receive blessings from God. I will hear some murmuring amongst them; it was a daunting task for them. They will grumpily go out for soul winning to fill the empty church pews with people. God desires servant who are willing and not people who are forced to do his work. Souls are won for Christ and it is done solely by the Holy Spirit. The Holy Spirit is not a slave driver, it is a gentle spirit.

Soul winning should even start in the Church. People are sent out to win souls outside and they come into the church and they are turned into something else and they become more frustrated and they have no peace at all. **In Matthew 23; 15 "Woe to you, teachers of the law and Pharisees, you hypocrites! You travel over land and sea to win a single convert, and when you have succeeded, you make them twice as much a child of hell as you are".** A soul will be won at Place A and you expect that soul to come to church at Place Z. Are we running recruitment agencies? Or it would have been better if that soul goes to a bible believing church around his or her locality. Huge bill boards and advertising platforms are spread all over the country when there is a church program to make money out of the people who flock there and the real message of receiving Christ is not made known to these people.

7. Using Sack Cloth

In some churches, the lead will tell its members to wear sackcloth and smear themselves with an ash that is the only way they can obtain riches and freedom. The leads even equate riches to freedom.

Sack cloth was used in the past as a sign for mourning or for repentance. Genesis 37: 34 "Then Jacob tore his clothes, put on sack cloth and mourned for his son many days.

Furthermore, when Joab and his brother Abishai murdered Abner because he had killed their brother Asahel in a battle, David was very disappointed that he told all the people that were with him to tear their clothes and put on sack cloth to mourn (2 Samuel 3)

Job also sewed sackcloth over his skin and turned his brow in the dust to mourn when he was facing hard times (Job 16). However, in the gospel of Christ, there is no usage of sack cloth, for we are saved by grace and not by works. Jesus is the high priest of the superior and new covenant. By calling this covenant new, he has made the first one obsolete; and what is obsolete and aging will soon disappear (Hebrews 8:13). More emphasis on the obsolete use of sack cloth is in Luke 10:13 "Woe to you, Korazin! Woe to you Bethsaida! For if the miracles that were performed in you had been performed in Tyre and Sidon, they would have repented long ago, sitting in sack cloth and ashes"

8. Leap Frog

In these Churches, you get a supposed miracle, something happens and you are back at where you began. Then you have to do something extraordinarily to get to another high point. God just want your heart and nothing more. The best miracle is Christ and whatever direction the Holy Spirit will blow you, you just move along.

9. Agugugaga (the gift of tongues)

You go to church these days and people learn the gift of tongues from their leads, the gift of tongues is a gift given to people by God through grace and not through works. For anyone who speaks in a tongue does not speak to men but to God. Indeed no one understands him; he utters mysteries of the spirit (1 Corinthians 14:2), speaking in tongues are for one's own edification not edifying the church.

Grace Not Works

When Elijah appealed to God against Israel: he said Lord, they have killed your prophets and torn down your altars; I am the only one left, and they are trying to kill me? God gave him his divine answer; I have reserved for myself seven thousand who have not bowed the knee to Baal. So too at the present time there is a remnant chosen by grace, and if by grace , then it is no longer by works; if it were, grace would no longer be grace. (Romans 11:3-6).

Hypothetically, we can have two groups of people, the "Gracers" and the "Workers". The workers sought earnestly but did not obtain because they felt works could achieve their goal, or better still Christ' already achieved goal, whereas, the" Gracers" believed in the word of God and rested in the finished work of Christ.

The workers were therefore hardened, as it is written God gave them a spirit of stupor, eyes so that they cannot see and ears so that they could not hear till this very day. (Romans 11:7).

So in effect any lead with a spirit of stupor is a worker and is not working under grace. I was invited to church one day. It was a hot Sunday afternoon; I just did not feel like going. However, this was a friend who had not invited me to any event ever so I felt I had to honor this invitation even though the odds were against me.

I hurriedly took a bath and wore a thin strapped dress and threw a shirt over, grabbed my bag and left. When I arrived, the lead had not arrived, so I joined in singing praises to God. Shortly after, the lead appeared and those who were not singing suddenly sung as if they had microphones. The voices were so loud and piercing that the melodious tune of one of my favorite gospel songs had turned into a discord. I had hard time trying to recognize that song. I realized that everyone wanted to be in the lead's good books.

Hmmm! The lead started his service and it was a "prophetic" service. All of a sudden, the lead lost control and it was like he was drunk. He had to be carried to his home; he could not finish the service. I quickly left for home; it was such a bizarre sight. The spirit of God is calm and gentle and not the other way round.

Prophecies

A young talented guy in our community died, out of the blue. Leads came out to say all sorts of things such as "I saw it" then I asked myself in solitude you saw it and what happened. The Power belongs to God only; you are just being used as a vessel to preach the gospel. Most Leads are not helping but rather worsening the problem by putting fear in the people hence a lot of people are afraid to attend church these days.

Peter's Vision

In Acts 10, there is an account of how God gives messages to people. A man called Cornelius saw an Angel of God, who told him his gifts to the poor have been remembered by God. So he should send men to Joppa to bring a man called Peter to his sent and Cornelius did just that.

Whilst the men were on their journey, Peter prayed and fell into a trance. He saw heaven opened and something like a large sheet containing all kinds of four footed animals. Then he heard a voice also saying; Get up, Peter, Kill and eat. He replied, surely not, for I have not eaten anything unclean or impure. This happened thrice.

As Peter was wondering the meaning of the vision, the spirit said to him that some men are looking for him; the spirit continued that he should go with them for he has sent them. So Peter went with the men to see Cornelius.

When Peter entered Cornelius house, there was a large gathering of people waiting for him. At that time it was against the law for a Jew to associate or visit a Gentile. But God's message became so clear here, that do not call anything impure or unclean for we are all one people. Cornelius told Peter of the message he has received from the Angel. Peter began to speak and he said "I now realize how true it is that God does not show favoritism but accepts from every nation the one who fears him and does what is right. "As Peter was preaching the gospel to the gathering, the Holy Spirit poured on all those who were gathered there and they spoke in tongues and praised God. There is no discrimination in the Lord; God is a God of peace!

In the past, God spoke to our forefathers through the prophets at many times and in various ways. But in these last days he has spoken to us by his son, whom he appointed heir of all things and through whom he made the universe (Hebrews 1:1-2).

Starting an interpersonal relationship with Christ is the first step so that we can hear his voice, listen to him and apply it to our lives. Not disregarding the fact that he at times gives messages to us through people but we have to discern in the spirit to know whether the message is from Christ or not.

There is a trend these days where some leads give messages to their members in public to receive cheers from people. Some predict the future using palmistry, astrology, metoposcopy (forehead reading) and other means other than Christ. Some leads ask you to raise your hand so that they can tell you what is going on in your life by reading your palms. Others read your forehead whilst talking to you, pick some cues and foretell your future.

However, the fact that someone can predict the future doesn't mean the person has the Holy Spirit.

In Acts 16:16-18. *Once when we were going to the place of prayer, we were met by a female slave who had a spirit by which she predicted the future. She earned a great deal of money for her owners by fortune-telling. She followed Paul and the rest of us, shouting, "These men are servants of the Most High God, who are telling you the way to be saved." She kept this up for many days. Finally Paul became so annoyed that he turned around and said to the spirit, "In the name of Jesus Christ I command you to come out of her!" At that moment the spirit left her. "Dear friends, do not believe every spirit, but test the spirits to see whether they are from God, because many false prophets have gone out into the world". (John 4:1)*

Prophecies are used as a tool of showmanship in churches these days. *But the one who prophesies speaks to people for their strengthening, encouraging and comfort.* (1 Corinthians 14:3). What is the use of all these prophecies if it causes unnecessary fear and panic in people? Some have the notion that the more you can see the more power you have. Everybody and the gift God has bestowed on him or her. It is not everybody who has been given the gift of vision.

Yes, God gives dreams and visions and trances but it is left to us to step into the spirit again and ask the giver for understanding and how to deliver the message. The way we see it and interpret it may be different and cause conflicts. Interpretation of the message is one major cause of conflicts in the victim's mind. Let love be your focus in delivering the message. "If you prophesy without love, don't prophesy. If you say it just as you are seeing it you can dampen the spirit of the person and you can send a wrong message. It also paves the way for people to fulfill the prophecy or act when it is out there in the public.

What you are seeing could be a word of knowledge and that message should rather be given to the person by calling the person aside not in the midst of people to show you have power. For all power and glory belongs to God.

Our goal in ministry is to make Christ great not making ourselves great and powerful. Sometimes, you even need to pray silently for God to give you the meaning of what you are seeing and turn it round positively into an advice for the person. Most leads interpret the prophecies with their own minds which put fear in the people involved. For example if it is divorce you are seeing, you can call the persons involved aside and teach them the way to Christ with the help of the Holy Spirit and word of God. For the word of God is sharper than any two edge sword which will help the couple to let go and live according to the spirit (1 Corinthians 13:1-*3)*.

If I speak in the tongues of men or of angels, but do not have love, I am only a resounding gong or a clanging cymbal. If I have the gift of prophecy and can fathom all mysteries and all knowledge, and if I have a faith that can move mountains, but do not have love, I am nothing. If I give all I possess to the poor and give over my body to hardship that I may boast, but do not have love, I gain nothing.

Placebo Effect

A Placebo is anything that looks like the real medical treatment but in actual fact it isn't. Placebo effect is used a lot in churches these days by leads.
These leads already see the vision that something has already occurred and they coerce members in paying huge sums of money to make it seem like your money made that thing happened. Yet his works has been finished since the creation of the world (Hebrews 4).

I once went to Church with my husband on a weekday; it was one of these prophetic services. My husband was expecting a check that afternoon. So the pastor saw my husband and said I see a check, God says sow a seed of a specified amount to push the check into your hands this afternoon. My husband looked at me and I smiled back.

We decided not to pay any money. The pastor kept on repeating it, we turned a deaf ear to it and we could see the disappointment on the pastor's face. Then he went on, if that money is not paid, the check will be withheld. We still did not budge. After church service, we entered our car and sped off to the company. His check had been ready since morning but they couldn't reach him. That was it for that church for my husband and me.

It is rather sad that lying, cheating and deceit has plagued the church. Leads are willing to do anything, even to the extent of compromising their values for money. You cannot serve God and money. Also, members are willing to do everything because their lead says so. What does God say? Why are we replacing God with a lead? These men of God have suddenly gained honors in psychology playing with the minds of the congregation. God doesn't need anything from you to help you. He just needs your heart that is all. Give your bodies as a living sacrifice; this is the true and proper worship.

There is another story of a banker who was seeking marriage found her way into a local church. She was a single woman in her 50's and very financially independent. A visiting pastor asked her to sow a seed of a huge amount for a quick marriage. She went and never came back. The pastor then followed her to her house and asked why she wasn't coming to church. She said she couldn't pay the mentioned amount and she is not comfortable with the church. Then the pastor said, you could have asked for reduction. I was alarmed at what I was hearing; suddenly the Church has become a market place where the Pastors have become shrewd businessmen. Amazing! Freely you have received and freely you will give.

Taxes on Paychecks

The smaller the amount, the less first fruit it is

The first money my friend Michael received at the beginning of the year was 3000 dollars. So he gave that money out to the lead as first fruit. The lead of his church was so happy and became Michael's best friend. The following year, Michael was not that lucky, he received 300 dollars at the beginning of the year and he gave that money to the lead as first fruit. The lead was so unhappy and said this is not first fruit. Michael was surprised, but this is the first money I received he explained. That year, the lead was not close to Michael anymore, till Michael eventually left the church.

Tithe before the Deed

Ava was in church one day, when the lead suddenly called her and told her God was about to give her money. His vision was that Ava was about to travel outside the country and that an organization will send her money for her ticket. In order to guarantee the money to come, Ava should pay a tenth of the total amount of money he saw as tithe to him. Ava was confused? What an order, if even she had to pay tithe, she had to receive the money first, not the other way round. Ava was reluctant at first but upon the lead's insistence, she paid that money. That was five years ago, I called Ava recently and we spoke at length, she still has not received any amount of money for any ticket whatsoever.

Genesis of Tithing

Melchizedek a priest of the most high blessed Abram and Abram **gave him a tenth** of everything. (Genesis 14:18-20). When God had revealed to Jacob that he was with him through his journey back to his father's house, he made a vow that, the Lord will be his God and of all that God will give him, he will **give him a tenth** (Genesis 28). He made that vow to God because he was so grateful for God's love for him. Furthermore, tithing was one of the commands that God gave to Moses on Mount Sinai for the Israelites. **"A tithe of everything from the land, whether grain** *from the soil or fruit from the trees, belongs to the Lord, it is holy to the Lord" (Leviticus 27:30).*

Setting the Levites Apart

When God struck the entire first born of Egypt down, he set the Levites apart for himself. The Levites were actually the first fruits of all the tribes of Israel. God said, **they are the Israelites who are to be given wholly to me** (Numbers 8:16). The Levites were set apart from the Israelites and purified to do God's work. The responsibility of the Levites was to assist their brothers (Aaron and Moses) in performing the duties at the tent of meeting (Numbers 8).

Genesis of first fruits

The Lord told Moses that when he enters the land given to him by God and God gives him the harvest that he reaps. He is to bring the priest a sheaf of the *first grain* and add a burnt offering; this is to ensure a lasting ordinance for the generations to come (Leviticus 23). At that time too, the *first born* of any animal belonged to the Lord (Leviticus 27:26).

What Tithing/ offerings/ first fruits were used for?

The offerings and first fruits which were regarded as holy were given to the Priests as their regular share. Accordingly, every male who was considered ceremoniously clean in that household could also eat it. **These offerings were not money but it was mainly produce of harvests**.

However, the Israelite Priests were told not to have any other inheritance in the land. *Then the Lord said to Aaron, "You will have no inheritance in their land, nor will you have any share among them; I am your share and your inheritance among them; I am your share and your inheritance among the Israelites." (Numbers 18:20)*

Tithing for the Levites

Since the Levites will receive no inheritance among the Israelites. God said: *I give to the Levites all the tithes in Israel as their inheritance in return for the work they do while serving at the tent of meeting (Numbers 18:22).* Then when the Levites receive the tenth of the Israelites offerings to God as tithe, they in turn must present a tenth of that tithe as the Lord's offering. These tithes are supposed to be presented to Aaron the priest, then the rest are supposed to be eaten by the Levites and their households for it is their wages for their work at the tent of meeting. (Numbers 18:25-30).

The Benefits of Tithes/ Offerings in the Old Covenant

Malachi 3:10-12 "bring the whole tithe into the storehouse, that there may be food in my house. Test me in this, says the Lord Almighty and see if I will not throw open the floodgates of heaven and pour out so much blessing that you will not have enough room for it. I will prevent pests from devouring your crops, and the vines in your fields will not cast their fruit, says the Lord Almighty. Then all the nations will call you blessed, for yours will be a delightful land, says the Lord Almighty".

Tithing/ Offerings was a law or covenant made by God to the Israelites at that time. In order to be in God's good books and reap all the benefits, all the tithes and the old covenant laws had to be fulfilled.

The New Covenant

Not that we are competent in ourselves to claim anything for ourselves, but our competence comes from God. He has made us competent as ministers of a new covenant—not of the letter but of the Spirit; for the letter kills, but the Spirit gives life (2 Corinthians 3:5-6)

Tithes and compulsory offerings were given to Levites and priests in order to fulfill the law. With the coming of Christ, that law has been fulfilled. "But the ministry Jesus has received is as superior to theirs as the covenant of which he is mediator is superior to the old one and it is founded on better promises (Hebrews 8:6) **Moreover, in the new covenant all believers of Christ are priests with Jesus being the high priest.**

Some may refer to Matthew 23:23 which read: woe to you, teachers of the law and Pharisees, you hypocrites! You give a tenth of your spices-mint, dill and cummin. But you have neglected the more important matters of the law- justice, mercy and faithfulness. You should have practiced the latter without neglecting the former. Meaning that at that time, the whole law should be practiced. People were rather dwelling on the benefits of the law and neglecting the most important aspects of the law and that is justice, mercy and faithfulness. However, at that time, Christ had not died, so the law was not fulfilled. With Christ's death, the law was fulfilled.

Old Testament laws have been fulfilled

Offering/ Tithes/ Seeds is not an obligation however people should give from their heart. The ritual practice of tithing used in churches to secure membership is wrong. Be shepherds of God's flock that is under your care, watching over them—not because you must, but because you are willing, as God wants you to be; not pursuing dishonest gain, but eager to serve; not lording it over those entrusted to you, but being examples to the flock. (1 Peter 5:2-3).

Some leads tell their members, if you do not pay tithe you will be sent to the pit of hell. Tithing is not the New Testament standard of giving. Christians are not under the Mosaic Law. *Jesus has been found worthy of greater honor than Moses, just as the builder of a house has greater honor than the house itself, for every house is built by someone, but God is the builder of everything. Moses was faithful as a servant in all God's house. Testifying to what would be said in the future. But Christ is faithful as a son over God's house. And we are his house, if we hold on to our courage and the hope of which we boast. (Hebrews 3:3-6).*

Freedom in Christ

Adwoba Addo-Boateng

Tithing was a law and Christ has set us free from all laws and covenant, so we ought to live as such. The Apostle Paul said we should stand firm as Christians and we should not let ourselves be burdened again by any form of slavery. Mark my words! I Paul, tell you that if you let yourselves be circumcised, Christ will be of no value to you at all. Again I declare to every man who lets himself be circumcised that he is obligated to obey the whole law. You who are trying to be justified by law have been alienated from Christ; you have fallen away from grace (Galatians 5). (Note that circumcision represents the law).

Moreover, giving should not be based on compulsion or to show off but should be done from the heart with an open mind and not expecting anything in return. Why did Jesus recommend the coins from the poor widow but did not recommend the huge money from the rich men at the temple (Mark 12). God loves a cheerful giver (2 Corinthians 9). In today's churches, giving has become so unhealthy that it has generated some kind of competition amongst members. If a lead wants to solicit for funds for a genuine cause, he or she could do it collaboratively with the church members genuinely and not be manipulative.

For instance, I was in church one day when the lead announced that" if you love me, give me this amount of money" this is absolutely manipulative. Obviously, everyone would want to be in the lead's good books, definitely they will give out that amount of money. What of the person who genuinely does not have? How would that person feel?

There was also an instance where a lead told a friend of mine to buy a car for his children to go to school in order to be blessed. Meanwhile this person has no means of transporting his own kids to school.

A church is supposed to uplift people and build them up in the faith of Christ. In addition, a church is not to make people any worse than when they came in.

Bribing God

The gift of God cannot be bought with money. When Simon saw that the gift of the Holy Spirit was been given to people by the Apostles, he offered money and Peter answered: "May your money perish with you, because you thought you could buy the gift of God with money! (Acts 8).

God doesn't need any money from us to bless us. These leads tag prices to everything from the sale of anointing oils to soaps for prophecies to be fulfilled. What of the grace that God has given us. If you feel like giving, give from your heart. Don't let anyone force you. Let's look at this scenario; do you give money to your father before he takes care of you? All what he requires is obedience even that he often shows mercy. In a situation when your father decides not to give you food because of some disrespect shown to him. He eventually let go and gives you food. All what matters is to have your heavenly father in your heart. If you are praying for something and it is not happening, don't try and bribe God. Wait for God's own time.

Fasting and Prayers

Fasting is giving up food for a period of time to focus on God; however fasting is backed by prayers which help us to focus entirely on God. There are instances in the bible where people fasted and prayed.

Prayer these days is like manual work, normally these leads have prayer points that the congregation all follow to pray. Praying in groups is not bad if the lead is being led by the spirit of truth. However, communicating with God every time to develop a personal relationship with God is paramount.

Hunger Strike!

There are times I have been to church where I have heard the lead telling members to fast for some duration, mostly against their will.

It is God who empowers us through his spirit to fast. Fasting is to humble yourself to get close to God and fasting goes with communication. Most times, the fasting is not backed by interpersonal relationship with God and our spirits are not in tuned with the fasting. I call them hunger strikes! Jesus fasted for 40 days and 40 nights as he was led by the spirit, the angels were there to strengthen him. Combining fasting with an intense focused time on prayer helps us to commune with God better. Most people look very down when fasting but Jesus told us to look radiant when we are fasting. "When you fast, do not look somber as the hypocrites do, for they disfigure their faces to show others they are fasting. Truly I tell you, they have received their reward in full. But when you fast, put oil on your head and wash your face, so that it will not be obvious to others that you are fasting, but only to your Father, who is unseen; and your Father, who sees what is done in secret, will reward you. (Matthew 6:16-18).

When we are led by the spirit to fast and pray we become more sensitive to his voice and we hear what he has to say and the spirit empowers us to fast for that period of time, even to the extent of disliking food.

Pay and Pray

I came across emergency prayers; I asked a friend, what is that? Then she said if you want God to answer your prayer quickly you pay and you pray. Wow! I was amazed, now we are bribing God. God works in His own time not your time. He makes all things beautiful in his own time. Can you tell God to answer you quickly because you have paid for a prayer to go through? I find it mind boggling. What of those who do not have money to pay? God only answers the rich. Funny! Then we are underrating him, He is a father to all who wants the best for all.

The Fateful Day

Ama entered her local church one day and by passed the usher at the gate in order to secure her favorite spot. She was so late today owing to the fact that she could not find her red checkered dress she so loved. She had an alternative anyway, but how she wished she was in that red checkered dress people admired when she walked by. Anyway, she was in church. She quickly sat down at that moment the lead was drawing near the pulpit. When he got there he shouted a big halleluyah! And the members of the congregation chorused a loud Amen mixed with smiles, laughter and clutter. Everyone was excited to see each other. The lead then proceeded with the sermon for that day. Then all of a sudden he was quiet, and then he called Ama out of the congregation and told her: he sees her husband dying very soon and that she should pay a huge sum of money to avert the death of her husband.

Ama was suddenly scared, how she wished she had not come to church that day. Was not finding her favorite dress, a wonderful stroke of luck or it was a sign of the Holy Spirit? She wished she had not come to church that day to hear all this. Is a prophecy or word of knowledge from the Holy Spirit supposed to cause fear and panic or it is to build people up in the faith of the Lord? She was totally disturbed and wished this day never was. What about the monetary aspect? How can she cough up that huge amount of money? Why are leads using fear, gimmicks to take money from people? No one can bribe God to do what he or she wants or avert something. God is sovereign and he does things according to his will. He sees the perfect picture that we do not see. Sometimes, death is even his way of ending misfortunes in one's life.

Oh, the depth of the riches of the wisdom and knowledge of God! How unsearchable his judgments, and his paths beyond tracing out! "Who has known the mind of the Lord? Or who has been his counselor?" "Who has ever given to God, that God should repay them?" For from him and through him and for him are all things. To him be the glory forever! Amen. (Romans 11:33-36)

Travel No More

In the olden times, people travel far and wide to see Jesus. However, we are more privileged today because God is in our midst. A time is coming when people will not travel to find me or worship me because I will be in their midst and worshippers will worship me in spirit and in truth. God just desires a genuine heart in order to worship him. Blessed are the pure in heart, for they shall see God.

The presence of God is not in the building; God's presence is around you. If you decide to pour your heart in the kitchen, the Holy Spirit comes around and you are in the presence of God.

Judgmental Prayers

Every Christian has a known and common enemy and that is the devil. When we choose to engage in practices such as judgmental prayers we are not allowing God to work in us for our lives to be fulfilled. Allow your guardian angel to work whilst you rest. Don't be a workman, for a workman always quarrels with his tools. Let God work for you by remaining in him and you will be fulfilled. (John 15) Fear is not of God, it is of the devil. Let's live in the Known that Christ died to save us from our sins

1 Thessalonians 5;15 says nobody pays back wrong for wrong but always strive to do what is good for each other and everyone else. An eye for an eye a tooth for a tooth was Moses law which has been replaced with a superior one. Jesus's message was all about love. He even said love your enemies, pray for them that spitefully hate you and persecute you. If we still have to pray judgmental prayers then we don't understand the gospel of Christ and his sufferings and crucifixion is useless. Moses law has been fulfilled through Jesus Christ the high priest sitting at the right hand of the father and interceding for us. There is no need to nail him over and over again on the cross.

Slam the door

Sin allows our relationship with God to dwindle. Sin pushes us farther away from God. How do we stay away from sin as Christians? We need to pray and live the word of God in order to have an interpersonal relationship with God so that the Holy Spirit will guide us. When we pray the Holy Spirit is activated in our lives and guides us in all our dealings.

We should also learn to forgive one another so that our prayers will go through. Yes, sometimes it is difficult to let go but when we allow God into our hearts, forgiveness is easy.

In Christ, there is love

When we put ourselves under the law we are falling from grace. For there are many rebellious people, more talkers and deceivers, especially those of the circumcision group and they must be silenced, because they are ruining households by teaching things they ought not to teach- and that for the sake of dishonest gain (Titus 1:11-12). Not that grace wasn't present at the time of the Old Testament, but Jesus Christ came with the ultimate manifestation of truth and grace. The Mosaic Law has been made obsolete and what is old and obsolete will completely pass away. (Hebrews).

Adwoba Addo-Boateng

CHAPTER 4
THE CRAFT OF HAIRDRESSING IS A GIFT FROM GOD

Spiritual Gifts/ Leading/Hairdressing

In 1 Corinthians 12: 4-8, The Apostle Paul said, "There are different kinds of gifts, but the same spirit distributes them. There are different kinds of service, but the same Lord. There are different kinds of working, but in all of them and in everyone it is the same God at work.

Now to each one the manifestation of the Spirit is given for the common good. One is given through the Spirit a message of wisdom, to another a message of knowledge by means of the same Spirit, to another faith by the same Spirit, to another gifts of healing by that one Spirit, to another miraculous powers, to another prophecy, to another distinguishing between spirits, to another speaking in different kinds of tongues, and to still another the interpretation of tongues. *All these are the work of one and the same Spirit, and he distributes them to each one, just as he determines"*. However, whatever gift you have, if you don't have love it profits you nothing.

We have different gifts, according to the grace given to each of us. If your gift is prophesying, then prophesy in accordance with your faith; if it is serving, then serve; if it is teaching, then teach; if it is to encourage, then give encouragement; if it is giving, then give generously; *if it is to lead, do it diligently*; if it is to show mercy, do it cheerfully. (Romans 12:6-8)

Leads in the Bible/ Biblical Hairdressers

There are leads in the Bible, who led people to their various destinations and worked diligently for God's purpose to be achieved. They allowed themselves to be greatly used by God, irrespective of the situation they found themselves in.

David

David as a little boy greatly relied on God for his victorious battle against Goliath although Goliath was the strongest physically (1 Samuel 17). Moreover, after removing Saul, (because he did not keep the Lord's commands) he (God) made David their king. God testified concerning him: 'I have found David son of Jesse, **a man after my own heart; he will do everything I want him to do**' (Acts 13:22). God paved a way for David to be king by creating a need for his services. He found favor with God and therefore he found favor with the King. Furthermore, David relied on the Holy Spirit through it all. He realized, he could not rule on his own, he submitted himself under God's rule for God's will to be done. Even though he faced many temptations and trials, he waited for the right time for God to take him out of the consequences through the sin he committed. After suffering his own consequences of sin, God restored him. David was God's friend and he abided in him until the end.

Joshua

When Moses died, God appointed Joshua to lead the Israelites to cross the Jordan River into the Promised Land given to them by God. He told Joshua, he was going to be with him and that he will never leave him. He told Joshua to be strong and courageous and to be obedient to the word of God. Joshua needed these attributes in order to be successful at leading. (Joshua 1). Joshua's obedience led him to crossing the Jordan River with the Israelites. In addition, Joshua's obedience to God led to the fall of the great city Jericho. When the Israelites acted unfaithfully in regard to the devoted things, the Lord's anger burnt against Israel. Joshua was discouraged when the Israelites were defeated by the men of Ai. Joshua prayed to the Lord and the Lord answered his prayer. A lead should therefore be prayerful and should consult God every step of the way. God told Joshua to consecrate the Israelites which he obeyed willfully and the Lord was with them again. (Joshua 7)

Gideon

Although God appointed Gideon to take up the role of a mighty warrior he was scared to take up that role and he asked for a sign. The Lord assured him that he was with him and that he should go in the strength that he has. This is emphasizing the fact that a leader should lead with the strength he has and that God will work through him and not the other way round (Judges 6). Furthermore, Gideon was also prayerful; he always sent his requests to God. ***Gideon said to God, if you will save Israel by my hand as you have promised- (Judges 6:36).*** Gideon also petitioned God: Then Gideon said to God, "Do not be angry with me. Let me make just one more request. Allow me one more test with the fleece. This time, make the fleece dry and the ground covered with dew" (Judges 6:39).

A leader should be prayerful, ***do not be anxious about anything, but in everything, by prayer and petition with thanksgiving, and present your requests to God. And the peace of God which transcends all understanding will guard your hearts and your minds in Christ Jesus. (Philippians 4:6-7).*** God asked Gideon to reduce the men for there were too many men. God did not want the Israelites to think that it was their works that gave them victory but we are victorious through grace. (In order not to be conceited, so that Christ's power may rest on us). Through it all, Gideon had an interpersonal relationship with God and communed with God all the time.

Moses

Moses had issues with anger; therefore he had to be prepared in order to be an effective leader. He one day saw an Egyptian beating a Hebrew, one of his own people. He was furious and took the law into his own hands and killed the Egyptian (Exodus 2:11-12). Apparently, someone saw the incident and eventually Pharaoh got to know of it and tried to kill Moses in return, but Moses fled to Midian. God prepared Moses in the wilderness for his role as a leader of the people by tending sheep. Through his tending of sheep he learnt some people management skills and he also became more appreciative of people and kind to others, which is one good attribute of a good leader. Moses also had an interpersonal relationship with God and communed with him all the time.

Through Moses' interpersonal relationship with God, Moses was able to tell God about his fears and his weaknesses. Moses said to the Lord, Oh lord I have never been eloquent, neither in the past, or since you have spoken to your servant. I am slow of speech and tongue". (Exodus 4:10). The Lord answered his prayer, *the lord said, now go; I will help you speak and I will teach you what to say.* (Exodus 4:12). This is in relation to what Paul said in 2 Corinthians 12:19 But he said to me, *"My grace is sufficient for you, for my power is made perfect in weakness." Therefore I will boast all the more gladly about my weaknesses, so that Christ's power may rest on me".* He told Jethro (father in law) about his return to Egypt and Jethro wished him well. Although God told him to go to Egypt, he found it necessary to inform his father in law. As such, he was also being respectful to earthly authority. (Exodus 4:18). Through it all, God was with Moses to achieve the goal of bringing the Israelites out of Egypt.

Hosea

Obedience to God: God loves the dirty

Luke 5:31 "Jesus answered them; "it is not the healthy who need a doctor, but the sick. I have not come to call the righteous, but sinners to repentance".

A lead should be obedient to God and put him or herself away, in order to achieve God's purpose. God told Hosea to marry an adulterous wife, because he wanted to show the people that he loves them no matter what. Hosea's wife committed adultery, but the Lord said to Hosea "Go show your love to your wife again, though she is loved by another and is an adulteress. Love her as the Lord loves the Israelites, though they turn to other gods and love the sacred raisin cakes (Hosea 3:1). That must have been hard for Hosea, it was not pleasant but he loved the Lord more than himself. He drew his sword and obeyed God and did as he was told.

Joseph

Joseph also tended sheep as a way of God preparing him to be a leader. Joseph was sold into slavery by his brothers. The Lord was with Joseph and he prospered, and he lived in the house of his Egyptian master (Genesis 39: 2). Joseph was ruled by the spirit of God and not by worldly desires. God was his focus, so he did not succumb to the desires of the flesh. He was falsely accused of rape and put in prison. All in all, the Lord was with him and the Lord's favor rested upon him and he succeeded in everything he did to the glory of Lord. *Now if we are children, then we are heirs—heirs of God and co-heirs with Christ, if indeed we share in his sufferings in order that we may also share in his glory (Romans 8:17)*.

Whilst in prison, the cup bearer and the baker wanted Joseph to interpret their dreams for them. They said: *We both had dreams, "they answered, but there is no one to interpret them." Then Joseph said to them, "Do not interpretations belong to God? Tell me your dreams" (Genesis 40:8).* Although Joseph had a gift of interpreting dreams, he relied solely on God for all interpretations; he acknowledged the fact that it was God who gives interpretation to dreams. God carved a way, for Joseph to get out of prison by using his gift at the right time. Accordingly, whatever gift God has given you, you have to confirm your calling, so that you will not be ineffective and unproductive in the Lord. *(2 Peter 1:3-8).*

Joseph was therefore put in charge of Egypt, a role designed for him by God. He had to go through all what he went through to prepare him for that role. When he became Governor of Egypt, he did not lord it over his brothers but rather welcomed them and lived at peace with them. This is one good quality of a good leader;

a leader should live at peace with all men irrespective of the situation and seek people's needs above his or hers.

The New Covenant

Jesus Christ

"Therefore Jesus said again, I tell you the truth, I am the gate for the sheep. All who ever came before me were thieves and robbers, but the sheep did not listen to them. I am the gate; whoever enters through me will be saved" (John 10:7-9).
Jesus was born into a very humble home and grew up doing ministry work at age thirty. He often went to the temple to preach and people marveled at his teaching. He was a great teacher who relied on the spirit of God, He taught in parables, however he was also tempted by the devil. When you are a lead, there will be temptations, but you have to cling to the Lord. 1 Corinthians 10:13 says *"No temptation has overtaken you except what is common to mankind. And God is faithful; he will not let you be tempted beyond what you can bear. But when you are tempted, he will also provide a way out so that you can endure it".*

When John the Baptist saw Jesus coming towards him, he said; *Look, the Lamb of God, who takes the sin of the world! ((John 1:29).* John then baptized him in order to fulfill all righteousness. As soon as Jesus was baptized, and a voice from heaven said, *"This is my son, whom I love; with him I am well pleased".* (Matthew 3:17). Jesus worshipped the Lord God and served him only. He performed many miracles yet he remained humble and obedient till the end. After his death, Jesus left us the Holy Spirit to guide us through our journey here on earth. (John 16:12). After Jesus was crucified on the cross, he finished the work that God his father gave him. He took away the sins of the world by nailing it on the cross.

We as Christians are supposed to believe in Jesus Christ, by submitting to his rule and living according to his word. *"Then they asked him, what must we do to do the work that God requires?*

Jesus answered, the work of God is this: to believe in the one he has sent (John 6:28-29). When we believe in Christ, we do all things in obedience to his word in order to be his children.

The Twelve Disciples

Jesus called out his twelve disciples to him and gave them authority to drive out evil spirits and to heal every sickness and disease. Jesus instructed them to go out **after the lost sheep** of Israel. He further told them to **preach the message of the kingdom** and tell the people, the kingdom of heaven is near. They should ***freely give as they have freely received***. Jesus further warned them of possible persecution "All men will hate you because of me, but he who stands firm to the end will be saved (Matthew 10:23) Confirming what Paul said in Romans 8:17 ***Now if we are children, then we are heirs—heirs of God and co-heirs with Christ, if indeed we share in his sufferings in order that we may also share in his glory.***

He also encouraged the disciples to be bold enough and not be afraid of men. In addition, they should be able to preach the word and not be intimidated by people ***"What I tell you in the dark, speak in the daylight; what is whispered in your ear, proclaim from the roots". (Matthew 10:27).***

In Matthew chapter 17, a man came to Jesus kneeling and asked him to have mercy on his epileptic son and that he brought his son to his disciples but they could not cure him. Jesus rebuked the demon and the boy was cured that very hour.
Then the disciples came to Jesus privately and asked him why they could not cast out the demon. Jesus then told them because of their unbelief. There was the need to have faith in whatever they were doing, how big your faith is will determine your outcome.

Jesus added that this kind of demon does not go out except by prayer or fasting. What is prayer, prayer is an interpersonal relationship with our heavenly father with love in your heart. What is fasting? Fasting is humbling yourself under God's mighty hand in order to get close to him. So we can conclude that in addition to faith, there is the need for the disciples to humble themselves under God's mighty hand and commune with him all the time therefore exhibiting the contrite heart for his will to be done.

Stephen

Stephen was a man who was chosen to help with the work of God (to serve tables and manage the distribution of food). He was chosen because he was a man of faith and led by the Holy Spirit. He was full of grace and used by God greatly to serve his people.

At a time, a group of people rose up and questioned Stephen about his talks to the people because they thought he was blaspheming God and Moses. Subsequently, they lodged a complaint against him to the council that he said that "Jesus will tear down this place and will change the traditions and customs which Moses handed over to us".

As Stephen stood in front of the council, they saw that Stephen's face was like an angel. With the Holy Spirit's lead, Stephen defended himself. The people were angry that Stephen was telling them that they did not obey the law and the Prophets who proclaimed beforehand the coming of the righteous one.

At that moment, he saw heaven opened up and the Son of Man standing at the right hand of God. They considered him guilty of blasphemy and they stoned him to death. As the people were stoning him, he prayed for them and asked God to forgive them. He was a faithful servant even until death and he was able to receive the crown of life. *Blessed is the one who perseveres under trial because, having stood the test, that person will receive the crown of life that the Lord has promised to those who love him (James 1:12).*

Saul turned Paul

In Acts 9:1-2 "Meanwhile Saul was still breathing out murderous threats against the Lord's disciples. He went to the high priest and asked him for letters to the synagogues in Damascus, so that if he found any there who belonged to the way, whether men or women, he might take them as prisoners to Jerusalem. Saul was persecuting the church without him knowing and he was called by God.

This signifies the fact that God can use anyone for his purpose. In Acts 9:15, when Ananias was complaining about the bad reports he had heard about Saul. *The Lord said to Ananias, "Go! This man is my chosen instrument to proclaim my name to the Gentiles and their kings and to the people of Israel.* Saul was then filled with the Holy Spirit and he began to preach in the synagogues that Jesus is the son of God. Paul then preached fearlessly in the name of Jesus and he really suffered for Christ. *The church throughout Judea, Galilee and Samaria enjoyed a time of peace. It was strengthened, and encouraged by the Holy Spirit, it grew in numbers, living in the fear of the Lord (Acts 9:31).*

Message of the Cross:

Promised rest for the weary

Jesus is the only lead or better speaking Lord, who promises us rest in all situations. Matthew 10: 28 say *"Come unto me all you who are weary and burdened and I will give you rest.* Furthermore, in order to enter this rest, we must believe and be obedient to his words and combine his message with faith. And to whom did God swear that they would not enter his rest if not to those who disobeyed? So we see that they were not able to enter because of unbelief. (Hebrews 3:18-19).

For the message of the cross is foolishness to those who are perishing, but to us who are being saved, it is the power of God. For it is written: "I will destroy the wisdom of the wise; the intelligence of the intelligent I will frustrate". (1 Corinthians 1:18-19). Therefore, since the promise of entering his rest still stands, let us be careful that none of you be found to have fallen short of it (Hebrews 4:1).

Drawing Your Sword

As a follower of Christ, you are supposed to draw your sword against the world, so that God will be your all sufficiency. *" Do not suppose that I have come to bring peace to the earth. I did not come to bring peace but a sword. For I have come to turn" a man against his father, a daughter against her mother, a daughter in law against her mother-in-law- a man's enemies will be the members of his own household" (Matthew 10:34).*

When God gave me a message to preach the gospel of Christ through writing, everyone thought I had lost it, especially people very close to me. I had to draw my sword against all their words and deeds. I stuck to God's plans for me and set my mind above (Colossians 3). Anyone who loves anything more than me, is not worthy of me. Whoever finds his life will lose it and whoever loses his life for my sake will find it (Matthew 10:39). I am living a fulfilled life now and I would not trade it for anything in the world.

CHAPTER 5

GOSH! THE HAIRDRESSER CUT OFF ALL MY HAIR

Characteristics of Bad" Leads"/ Hairdressers

God of Men

These men of God tend to play God and feel they are "all knowing" with super strength. Humility is one attribute of a man of God which is clearly missing from their dictionaries. They claim the glory of God at any prayer said. There was a time when a sister was in labor, and then her husband called the pastor to inform him. The wife had one of the easiest births ever, it was so smooth. Then the next minute, he heard that the lead was claiming the glory by saying that it was a very difficult birth and if they had not called him they would have lost the baby. This was clearly not the case. Why are we trying to take the glory of God?

They don't freely give

I was in Church one day when the lead asked a lady to pay an amount of money in order to pray for her. I was totally astonished. Jesus asked his disciples to go after the lost sheep of Israel and do the work freely as they have freely received (Matthew 10). And if we claim we are followers of Christ, we need to imitate Christ.

They alter true worship

A friend, moved to a new house. She then called her lead to come and sanctify the house before she moves in. The lead came to pray in the new house and said that he has built an altar in the new house for her. The lead further added that when my friend is moving to a new house, she should call him, so that he can come and remove the altar to the new house. I found it bizarre; the altar is your heart and nothing else

The altar is your heart in the new covenant. This is the covenant I will make with them after that time, says the Lord. I will put my laws in their hearts, and I will write them on their minds." (Hebrews 10:16). Your heart is a determinant of your true worship with Jesus Christ. There was a time in Church when people were asked to put money on the altar and that the altar will speak for them. If you put your money on the altar and it is not coming from your heart then it is not true worship. Worshippers that our heavenly father desires are those who worship him in spirit and in truth.

Destroying families, marriages and relationships

Aba was a lovely girl; she was always in high spirits. She attended her local church and she was an usher. She was very patient with the people and she always made sure the members were comfortable sitting in the pews.

She was one day invited to another church by her friend, she honored the invitation. She saw how beautiful the church was and said to herself, surely, the good lord lives here! As soon as she entered, the lead called her and said she sees her dying. She was suddenly struck down with fear. She was willing to do everything that the lead will say to avert her so called death. The lead gave her some concoction of oil and other substances to drink which she did.

Afterwards, Aba became engrossed in the church that she never listened to her parents anymore. Her family has been replaced with the church. Aba was hardly at home, she was always at church. She one day came home and packed all her belongings and never returned. She was staying in the church, owing to the fact that the lead told her she should be in the presence of God always. Let me say this, anywhere you decide to call on the name of God, you activate the Holy Spirit and that place becomes sanctified with God's presence. God is everywhere.

Aba's relationship with her family and friends deteriorated. Eventually, Aba was diagnosed with a strange illness and the same family and friends that she neglected were the only ones that came to her aid and the lead was nowhere to be found. God gave us families on earth to give us love and support that we need in our journey on earth. Families are special and are designed by God; they are there to help us. A lead is supposed to be unifying not causing divisions amongst people.

Bombshell

Being a habitual late comer, I quickly dashed into church one hot afternoon an hour past the opening time. The pastor was already preaching when I walked in. I quickly smiled at my friend Sarah, she quickly smiled back. Sarah was my friend who introduced me to this church, just to let you know. My big sister in church business, I will call her. I sat at the end of the row and put my bag on my lap, as I did not want to put my bag on the floor. Suddenly, a man in his mid-fifties walked into the church with a big frown on his face. He walked straight to the pulpit and snatched the microphone from the Pastor. Where is security? I enquired.

Everyone sat still as the man narrated his story of how the Pastor has held his wife captive. He went further to state that his wife is hardly at home owing to the fact that she is always at church. The wife is very disrespectful to him and wonders the kind of teaching been given in the Church. It was a -tell- all session with revealing incidents. Oh my! It was as if I was in a drama club, the scene was acted out so beautifully. I marveled at the depth of information and it gave me insights of how the church was affecting relationships especially marriages instead of helping to build them up.

Obviously, that man was not enjoying married life; his marital life has becoming something else with the wife always in Church to pray for a supposed break through. Wives, submit yourselves to your own husbands as you do to the Lord. For the husband, is the head of the wife as Christ is the head of the church, his body, of which he is the Savior. Now as the church submits to Christ, so also wives should submit to their husbands in everything. (Ephesians 5:22-24).

Three is a crowd

Marriage is a union between a man and a woman with God being the head. In our daily struggles with our marriages we should look up to Christ and stem towards unconditional love for our partners. Sometimes, loving our partners in the midst of suffering is difficult and we tend to leads for advice on how to "marry". There is absolutely nothing wrong with that if it is a godly advice but when all our attention shifts from Christ to these leads then it becomes a huge problem.

These leads then become the head of the marriage and it can get so bad that whatever decision you take you have to inform the lead. Your spouse gets relegated to the background then it looks as if you are marrying the lead rather.

If you need any advice or wisdom, God is there to give it to you if we ask him in prayer. (James 4). Some leads interference in marriages stem out from the fact that we allow it. We need to submit to God's rule whilst praying so that he can rule over our lives.

No problem is bigger for God to solve, if we involve him in our marriages. Sometimes these leads come out with some supposed visions about your partner or spouse. Some of these visions make you hate your partner and before you know it you are drifting away from the marriage that God instituted and already creating another marriage.

Some of the leads acts good or better than your spouse from what you tell them, then you begin to think that they are a better partner than your husband. It can even get to the extent of lusting after the lead. Then, after desire has conceived, it gives birth to sin; and sin, when it is full-grown, gives birth to death. (James 1:15).

A lady was having problems in her marriage and turned to a lead for comfort. The lead told her all sorts of things about her husband. The lady in turn reacted negatively to the information that she received from the lead and the marriage was turning sour. The lead suddenly took over the marriage and will tell the lady what to do and what not to do. The lady unknowingly was having a soft spot for the lead and things were taking a different turn. She was seeing the best in the lead and now unconsciously she was wishing that the lead was her husband.

Her husband will come home after work and she will be so busy on phone calls with this lead, paying no attention to the husband. Sometimes she wishes the husband will go away so she could talk to this person. God was definitely left out of the picture and instead of the lady having an interpersonal relationship with God; she was having an interpersonal relationship with the lead. The relationship was getting worse. The pastor has become the lady's all dependency and the place was getting too crowded for God to come in.

The lady realized that she was also submitting to this lead rather than submitting to her husband. Wives submit yourselves to your husbands as it is fitting to the Lord (Colossians 3:18). After a while, the lady was beginning to be uncomfortable with this relationship that she decided to pray to God to help her.

Then God came in, she realized she had made a fool out of herself. When the Holy Spirit was activated in her, she realized she had made this lead her all dependency and that was totally wrong. But the Advocate, the Holy Spirit, whom the Father will send in my name, will teach you all things and will remind you of everything I have said to you. (John 14:26).

God is the only one who can save your marriage through having an interpersonal relationship with him and living according to the spirit. If he chooses to give you advice through someone, he will but do not depend on anyone for advice. The lady begun to love her husband and their marriage was restored. The lead is unto the next victim. Beware!!! For lack of knowledge my people perish!

Sermons

Sermons are heavily shifted to the righteousness of the law and prosperity instead of on Christ. The law is only a shadow of the good things that are coming—not the realities themselves. For this reason it can never, by the same sacrifices repeated endlessly year after year, make perfect those who draw near to worship. Otherwise, would they not have stopped being offered? For the worshipers would have been cleansed once for all, and would no longer have felt guilty for their sins. But those sacrifices are an annual reminder of sins. It is impossible for the blood of bulls and goats to take away sins.

The Holy Spirit also testifies to us about this. First he says:

"This is the covenant I will make with them after that time, says the Lord. I will put my laws in their hearts, and I will write them on their minds. "Then he adds: "Their sins and lawless acts I will remember no more." And where these have been forgiven, sacrifice for sin is no longer necessary. (Hebrews 10: 16-18)

Moreover, these sermons are also skewed to how one is to remain faithful to his church and lead not God. I think that the lead should set a good example to the members of the church by being loyal to the members first (Jeremiah 23). A lead should be loyal to its flock by being truthful to them.

"'Love the Lord your *God with all* your *heart and with all* your *soul and with all* your *mind. And* the *second is like it: 'Love your neighbor as yourself'*". In Mark chapter 10 verse 17 to 27, we are told of the story of the rich man and the kingdom of God.

The rich man wanted to enter the kingdom of God but he wasn't willing to part away with his wealth. He obeyed the commandments of God and he was righteous but he worshipped his wealth. When you give to the poor you are giving to God. 'Truly I tell you, whatever you did for one of the least of these brothers and sisters of mine, you did for me.' (Matthew 25:40).

This scripture tells us that when wealth is given to us we are supposed to share it to the underprivileged.

Christianity is not a means to financial gain

If anyone teaches otherwise and does not agree to the sound instruction of our Lord Jesus Christ and to godly teaching, they are conceited and understand nothing. They have an unhealthy interest in controversies and quarrels about words that result in envy, strife, malicious talk, evil suspicions and constant friction between people of corrupt mind, who have been robbed of the truth and who think that godliness is a means to financial gain.

But godliness with contentment is great gain. For we brought nothing into the world, and we can take nothing out of it. But if we have food and clothing, we will be content with that. Those who want to get rich fall into temptation and a trap and into many foolish and harmful desires that plunge people into ruin and destruction. For the love of money is a root of all kinds of evil. Some people, eager for money, have wandered from the faith and pierced themselves with many griefs. (1Timothy 6:3-10)

Sharing is Loving

In 2 Kings Chapter 4, there was an account of Elisha and the woman from Shunem. This woman always gave Elisha food whenever he passes by. So she told her husband one day that they should make a small room for him so that whenever he passes by, he can sleep there as well. And the husband agreed. So anytime, Elisha passed by he will turn in there. Elisha was so pleased with the Shunammite woman's hospitality that out of gratefulness, he asked the woman what he can do for her. So Elisha had the information that she had no child. Elisha called her and told her that "about this time next year, you will embrace a son". The woman conceived and bore her son. When she was helping Elisha and sharing her home with him, she had no idea that she will receive her heartfelt desire. She had what she had always wanted by going all out to help a total stranger. Although, her son was a gift from God, she encountered many problems (1 Corinthians

10:13). At the end of it, she was victorious in the end when she put her trust in God.

Oppressing the poor

Moneys from the church that are to be used for the welfare of orphans, widows and strangers, however, these orphans and widows and the poor are rather exploited "Then the righteous will answer him, 'Lord, when did we see you hungry and fed you, or thirsty and gave you something to drink? When did we see you a stranger and invited you in or needing clothes and clothe you? When did we see you sick or in prison and went to visit you? "The King will reply, 'Truly I tell you, whatever you did for one of the least of these brothers and sisters of mine, you did for me.' (Matthew 25:37-40). We should rather encourage the disheartened, help the weak and be patient with everyone.

The "poor" also want to be blessed.

Prophetic services are so entertaining and so dramatic and it is always best when you are an observer. I attended a church service one afternoon, I was a guest member or so I will call it. I always made cameo appearances here and there because I happen to know the lead of that church. During this special service, the lead asked those who want to be blessed to take a "special" chair and sit down. People rushed for those special chairs, and sat on it. The lead then scanned through those who possessed the special chairs and ordered some "poor" people to leave those special chairs and go to their seats. I thought to myself quietly. The "poor" also want to be blessed. The lead went on and said those who took the special seats should pay an amount of money. I nearly burst into laughter; I now understand why the" poor" was made to sit down on their original seats. They obviously, could not pay that amount of money to fill the lead's pocket.

The sheep and the goats

The shepherd Jesus will separate the sheep from the goats when he comes in his glory. What should we do as children of God to be in the sheep category? For I was hungry and you gave me something to eat, I was thirsty and you gave me something to drink, I was a stranger and you invited me in, I needed clothes and you clothed me, I was sick and you looked after me, I was in prison and you came to visit me (Matthew 25:34). How can you say you love God when you do not love your brother or sister, God is love (1 John 4:20). When you do these things for the least of all people, you do for God and you receive eternal life.

Offertory/Seed Sowing

Offer your bodies as a living sacrifice; this is a true and proper worship. Our bodies are the best seed to God. We should try and live according to the word of God, for this is pleasing in God's eyes.

Before we sow "financial" seeds our consciences are appealed to by these leads that the seed will give us some sort of economic profits. God will not give you a gift, when you are not prepared for it, other than that it might destroy you. You cannot bribe God with seeds in order to gain financial blessings.

John attended a local church, where he was forced by the lead to sow his car for a supposed financial blessing. He felt, why sow my car as a sacrifice in order to gain. Jesus Christ has already sacrificed his life for us, once and for all. The blood of Jesus cleanses us from all sins and we do not need to nail him on the cross over and over again. All we have to do is to believe in him.

He gave his car out since he was desperate for financial blessings. He never received any financial blessings till date. It was a talk amongst the people in the town. The lead realized, his church was being talked about and it could go against him. He quickly came to church to give an announcement that John did not receive his supposed financial blessing because he changed the car and he did not bring the car on time.

We should stop deceiving ourselves, for God is not mocked. *Every good and perfect gift is from above, coming down from the*

Father of the heavenly lights, who does not change like shifting shadows. (James 1:17)

Another lead also told his ushers to contribute and buy a car for him to drive. He quoted huge sums of money for them to pay. Meanwhile some were struggling to make ends meet. The ushers felt if they did not pay, they will not be liked by the lead. Some even borrowed money to pay. Why are we oppressing the poor?

Everyone must be willing to part with a gift he or she already has not according to what one does not have and they have the free will to do that. **The ministry of Christ does not seek to relieve others to overburden others but to promote equality amongst people (2 Corinthians 8: 12-13).**

The Dollar Notes

Ama slammed the door behind her and there was a loud bang! She was heading to church; she was running late, she was the lead's secretary. Ama got to church few minutes before the pastor arrived. Thank God, she got there just in the nick of time. The service started with the usual testimony time, prayer time and praises time. Everyone was waiting for the climax of the service which was the prophetic time.

When the pastor started the prophetic "demonstration", Ama was so happy, that was her favorite part too. The lead called a few people and told them what was going to happen in their lives, the congregants cheered along! After a while the lead said some people have some dollars in their bags, God wants you to give him that money. Two "obedient" people got up and gave the pastor the money.

Ama had some money in her bag, that she plans paying the children's school fees. Are we now been compelled to give? She decided not to take the money; she had school fees to pay. The lead still wasn't satisfied with what he had gotten so far, so he went on and on that there is someone holding on to his or her money and doesn't want to give it to God.

Ama still did not budge; she had fees to pay, period! Ama heard her name called by the lead; she thought the lead needed her to help him with something. The lead called out her name so loud that Ama got up with so much anxiety.

The pastor continued Ama, do you want God to bless you? Hello, who doesn't? That is why we are all here, Ama thought to herself. The lead went on, God said; you should give that money in your bag to him, so that doors will open for you. Now, Ama has given up, everyone was staring at her.

Ama went into her already opened bag, pulled the dollar notes out reluctantly and gave it to the lead. That month, she could not pay the kids fees and she felt she had been duped. Under no circumstances, should a lead force you to do things against your will. Your will is something God himself will not take from you. We are all at liberty to do whatever we want to do. The spirit of God, never holds anyone captive, **God also loves a cheerful giver!**

The Call

I was at home one day when a lead called me, after the usual pleasantries, the lead said, God wants him to sow a seed of a specified amount but he doesn't have the money. He went on to say, as he was praying, God told him to ask me. The first question, I asked was really, God said ask me. I replied back with a question.

Honestly, I did not have that amount of money anywhere. So, you see the way they use tricks and playing with the mind all in the name of God. If I had that amount of money, that would have been it, but because I didn't have that amount of money and God is "all knowing", I immediately knew he was lying.

Adwoba Addo-Boateng

U.N. Employed

A lady I knew had been praying for a job ever since she finished school, but she wasn't getting any job. Every time, some leads will foretell her future by telling her about some non-existence jobs that never came to pass. And anytime, these words of knowledge fail, the leads will come up with an excuse one way or the other as to why the word of knowledge never came to pass. The excuses were mainly because she didn't pay some financial commitment.

What does God require from us to give us something? What, then, shall we say in response to these things? If God is for us, who can be against us? He who did not spare his own Son, but gave him up for us all—how will he not also, along with him, graciously give us all things? (Romans 8:31-32).

This lady still had hope that one day she will get a job. On one fateful day, she checked her email and realized that she had an offer letter from an international job she applied two years ago. Her joy knew no bounds; the first person she called was her lead. I have got a job she shouted! The lead said we thank God! How much is the pay? The lead added. The lady in a happy mood mentioned the salary which was thousands of dollars. The next Sunday, the lead announced it in church and told the congregants of how he prayed and prayed and God finally gave the lady a job.

Everyone was so happy in church that day; it was the new topic in town. The lady started preparing towards her travel since she was to be stationed in another country, with respect to that she had to make a new passport for herself and her family since their passports had expired a long time ago.

She started the process and for some reason the passports were delaying and her time for her departure was approaching. She called the lead to help her in prayers since she believes the devil was at work. The day set for her departure passed without her getting her passports, now frustration had set in. she channeled all her energy to church praying so that she could have her passport, so she can finally work.

Months passed and everyone was asking what she was still doing around. In a surprising turn of events, the passports came and the employer told her to pay for her rent in the new country since they could not cater for that. It was then that she realized her job was a scam after all. She went to the same organization's website and she saw a sample of the offer letter she received as scam and the general public was being cautioned.

She quickly told the lead about the whole situation. Now, how to denounce that testimony has become a strong hurdle to cross for the lead. Well, he had to do it anyway because people were asking questions. Guess what he told the congregants, your guess is as good as mine. He told the congregants that because the lady's passport delayed, the organization had pushed her employment to next year, and that the lady will start work next year. What a shame! Lying to keep your members in Church! The lady was so disappointed that she left the church. She started her own company and she is doing really well.

The power does not belong to us but to God, when we want to take the glory of our prayer doing something for someone then we are not getting it. Where is the Christ factor in this story? I leave it to your discretion.

Physical/Verbal Abuse

Loyalty to God is downplayed whilst loyalty to the lead and the Church is overemphasized. In churches these days, it is how loyal you are to your lead that counts. Some churches preach that no matter what your lead is doing, you still have to exhibit some sort of loyalty. Even if he or she misleads the flock, you still should be a loyal member. The church does not define you. Loyalty to God and how you walk in his ways is what counts and matter to God.

Some leads abuse their members physically and verbally all in the name of miracles. The spirit of God is a gentle spirit. There was a time when I entered a local church and the lead was raining insults on the members for coming to church late. I found it very appalling. A lead should be able to walk the talk and set good examples for his members to follow.

Jesus is a cool dude!

I went to church one day when the lead was shouting on top of his voice and telling his members how angry he was. He further revealed that someone had threatened to kill his church member because of a position at work. So he is so angry and that he had said some prayers and the man who threatened his church member with killing him is now mad.

He concluded that the God he serves has repaid him for his evil deeds. Will Christ kill for a position? Jesus himself said, love your enemies, bless them that curse you and pray for them that spitefully hate you. Through imitating Christ, people who do not know Christ can get to know Christ through the examples we live here on earth.

Favoritism

During Church service one day, a man dressed in fine clothes entered the church, this was his first time visiting. Immediately, the lead saw how nicely dressed he was, he immediately gave him a seat at the high table then afterwards a woman dressed up in rags entered the church, you could see that the woman was really in distress. The woman sat down at the front row and the Lead told the woman to get up and move to the back and that the seat was reserved.

There is a story of an old man who entered a church in tattered clothes. He sat at the front pew since he was early. When the ushers came in they told him to move back since he was shabbily dressed and allow the people that are finely dressed to occupy the front seats. As the people kept coming in, he kept on moving back till he got to the last pew. Unfortunately, more people came in and he had to sit outside the church building because the church was so full of finely dressed people. Whilst this man was seated outside, a young man who was obviously late came to sit by him. The young man talked of how he always wanted to enter the church but he was always late. The old man told the young man of how he was also trying to enter the church but was unsuccessful, the young man asked the old man, and who are you. The old man said" Jesus"

My brothers and sisters, believers in our glorious Lord Jesus Christ must not show favoritism. Suppose a man comes into your meeting wearing a gold ring and fine clothes, and a poor man in filthy old clothes also comes in. If you show special attention to the man wearing fine clothes and say, "Here's a good seat for you," but say to the poor man, "You stand there" or "Sit on the floor by my feet," have you not discriminated among yourselves and become judges with evil thoughts?

Greed

A lead took a man's house and said it was a sacrifice God had commanded him to do. This man gave out his house against his family's will. He told the man that in seven months, his life will change. He will get a good job and relocate with his family to live outside the country. The supposed blessing was not forthcoming for years. All of a sudden, then he came up with another excuse why the supposed blessings were not coming. The supposed blessing never came and the man got ill and died out of frustration.

Characteristics of a Good Leader/Hairdresser

Everybody and how he or she was born to do. Some are born to lead and others are born to be subordinates, whichever way you just have to place the lord first in whatever you do.

> ➢ A leader must seek wisdom in all he or she does. *If* any of *you* lacks *wisdom, you* should *ask God*, who gives generously to all without finding fault, and it will be given to *you*. (James 1:5)

- A leader must be hospitable, one who loves what is good, who is self-controlled, upright, holy and disciplined and he or she must hold firm to the truthful message as taught by the holy spirit, so that he can encourage others by the sound doctrines and refute others who oppose it (Titus 1:8)

- A leader must love above all things, Love and faithfulness keep a king safe; through love his throne is made secure. (Proverbs 20:28). A leader must be compassionate. The parable of the Good Samaritan shows the extent of love in action. When we have love then we can have compassion on others.

- A leader must seek for God's approval not man's approval. The Apostle Paul in his letter to the Galatians said "Am I now trying to win the approval of human beings, or of God? Or am I trying to please people? If I were still trying to please people, I would not be a servant of Christ.

- As a prisoner for the Lord, then, I urge you to live a life worthy of the calling you have received. Be completely humble and gentle; be patient, bearing with one another in love. (Ephesians 4).

- A leader must be in submission to God. Even Jesus as Lord as he is, he was in total submission to God's will (Here I am, O Lord! I have come to do thy will) Hebrews 10:5

CHAPTER 6

THE BEST HAIRDRESSER IS CHRIST!

Turning on the Light

In him was life and that life was the light of all mankind. (John 1:4). When a place is dark and there is something in front of you, you cannot see, but when you put on the light you can find it because the light makes you see. Also, when you go to your home one day and there is a power cut, you sleep in darkness but when it happens continuously you go to the source and find out what the problem is.

Putting on the light is searching the scriptures, reading and allowing the Holy Spirit to guide us in living according to his will. Of course, when we put on that light we imitate Christ in every way by putting on love. And when we put on that light, darkness varnishes. The light shines in the darkness, and the darkness has not overcome it (John 1:5)

 Love covers a multitude of sins, when we love no matter what we do not engage in so many things that are not in line with Christ, we put away the sins of the flesh (Galatians 5).Let your light so shine, so that people may see your good works and glorify your father which is in heaven. Let the light in you radiate so much that it benefits all others by loving your neighbor as yourself. If your light is dim, how will others around you see? When Jesus spoke again to the people, he said, "I am the light of the world. Whoever follows me will never walk in darkness, but will have the light of life." (John 8:12).We must put on the light, in order to find our divine purpose and for God to fulfill that divine purpose through us.

The Ministry is a result of the Spirit of the Living God

The anointed ones are those who have received Christ as their personal savior written not with ink but with the Spirit of the living God, not on tablets of stone but on tablets of human hearts.
Such confidence we have through Christ before God.

Not that we are competent in ourselves to claim anything for ourselves, but our competence comes from God. He has made us competent as ministers of a new covenant—not of the letter but of the Spirit; for the letter kills, but the Spirit gives life. (2 Corinthians 3)

Freedom in Christ

Now the Lord is the Spirit, and where the Spirit of the Lord is, there is freedom. (2 Corinthians 3:17) It is for freedom that Christ has set us free. Stand firm, then, and do not let yourselves be burdened again by a yoke of slavery (Galatians 5:1).

Holy Spirit is the Helper

"But the Advocate, the Holy Spirit, whom the Father will send in my name, will teach you all things and will remind you of everything I have said to you". (John 14:26).

The Miracles of Jesus:

The Man with Leprosy

Jesus healed the man with leprosy with a touch when he was willing and desired the healing. Jesus reached out his hand and touched the man, I am willing, he said be clean! Immediately he was cured off his leprosy (Matthew 8:3).

The Centurion's Servant

In another account, a centurion wanted Jesus to heal his servant and he had so much faith in Jesus' words that Jesus words will heal his servant. Then Jesus said to the centurion, Go! It will be done just as you believed it would. And his servant was healed at that very hour (Matthew 8:13). There is power in God's words.

The Fever of Peter's Mother in law

Peter's mother in law was sick and down with fever. They called on Jesus and He touched her hand and the fever left her, and she got up and begun to wait on him (Matthew 8:15).

Driving Out Spirits

He drove out spirits with a word and healed all the sick (Matthew 8:16). Accordingly, He also drove out demons from possessed men who were behaving violently. (Matthew 8:28-34)

Jesus Calms the Storm

When he was with his disciples on the boat, a furious storm came up on the lake and swept over the boat, but he rebuked the winds/ waves and it was completely calm (Matthew 8:28-34).

Jesus heals the Paralytic Man

In Matthew 9, there is an account of how Jesus healed the paralytic man by saying "Get up and take your mat and go home. Take heart, your sins are forgiven.

The Woman with the Issue of Blood

The woman had faith that if she touched the hem of Jesus garment, she will be healed. The woman with the issue of blood touched the hem of his garment and he was made whole. Jesus turned and saw her, take heart daughter he said; your faith has healed you. And the woman was healed from that moment (Matthew 9:22).

Jesus Heals the Blind

The blind men asked Jesus for mercy and they had faith and believed that Jesus could heal them. Then he touched their eyes and said according to your faith will it be done to you. (Matthew 9:29)

Characteristics of Christ's Lead/ Christ's Trained Hairdressers

> *Live According to the Spirit*

A servant of God should refrain from sins of the flesh and live according to the spirit of God. Those who are led by the spirit of God are sons of God. (Romans 8:14). These sins of the flesh can be found in Galatians 5:19-21 which reads ***the acts of the flesh are obvious: sexual immorality, impurity and debauchery; idolatry and witchcraft; hatred, discord, jealousy, fits of rage, selfish ambition, dissensions, factions and envy; drunkenness, orgies, and the like. I warn you, as I did before, that those who live like this will not inherit the kingdom of God***. Accordingly, the mind governed by the flesh is death, but the mind governed by the Spirit is life and peace. The mind governed by the flesh is hostile to God; it does not submit to God's law, nor can it do so. Those who are in the realm of the flesh cannot please God. (Romans 8:6-11)

Bearing the Fruits of the Spirit:

The fruits of the spirit are the attribute a person bores if he has the Holy Spirit.

Humility

The king of peace was given birth in a manger in a horse stable that was a great sign of humility. During the Lord's last supper a dispute arose amongst the disciples as to who was the greatest. Jesus gave us the attribute of a good servant in Luke 22: 27 **"But you are not to be like that. Instead, the greatest among you should be like the youngest, and the one who rules like the one who serves.** For who is greater, the one who is at the table or the one who serves? Is it not the one who is at the table? But I am among you as one who serves".

Jesus himself taught us that if you are greater, then you should serve the most. Zaccheus a rich tax collector humbled himself to climb the sycamore tree in order to see Jesus. He did not let his height be a limitation to see Christ. He wanted to see Christ at all cost. He was ready to serve the Lord by seeking first his kingdom and all His righteousness, by willing to sell half of his possessions and give to the poor and also to pay back money for all his wrong doings. Jesus said to him in Luke 19:9-10 that "Today salvation has come to this house, because this man, too, is a son of Abraham for the Son of Man came to seek and to save the lost."

Dedicated

The Parable of the ten virgins signifies that when God gives you a task you are supposed to put your all into it. When you are faithful with a few things God entrusts you with. He entrusts you with more things and you share in his happiness. He again offers you rich rewards freely because you have done your part.

When the bridegroom that is Jesus appears, will your oil run out? Or you will have enough oil to wait for his arrival? How do we make sure our oil does not run out? The answer lies in 2 peter 1:5-8 to confirm our calling and election. For this reason, we should make every effort to add to your faith goodness; and to goodness, knowledge; and to knowledge, self-control; and to self-control, perseverance; and to perseverance, godliness; and to godliness, mutual affection; and to mutual affection, love.

For if you possess these qualities in increasing measure, they will keep you from being ineffective and unproductive in your knowledge of our Lord Jesus Christ

Peacemaker

When interacting with humans everywhere, conflict naturally emerges. Normally, this is due to the fact that individuals from different backgrounds and orientation are working together to complete a task.

Moreover, it is hard to avoid conflicts entirely, owing to the fact that everyone has its own opinions, values, perceptions and needs. There is therefore, the need to manage conflicts so as not to destroy our relationship with people. Therefore, a lead is to ensure peace amongst all people. ***Blessed are the peacemakers, for they will be called children of God***. (Matthew 5:19)

Compassionate

I hurriedly entered a church service one day because I was late and did not want to miss the sermon. I sat down by a sick man who was groaning and moaning in pain. Apparently, he was dying and had come to the church for the first time to be healed. The lead was preaching at that time, but the moaning and groaning was so loud that the lead was distracted.

Then he asked angrily, who is that interrupting my sermon? I am preaching! Then a middle aged lady who had accompanied the sick man to church, shouted: My Uncle is dying? The lead paid no attention to her frantic calls. He continued with his preaching and the congregation followed the sermon in agreement. The lady kept on shouting and she was not paid attention to. The lead's response was, you only come to church because of healing or miracles and you disturb the whole congregation with your issues. I was taken aback, what is a lead for?

We have all been given chances. God put you in this position so that you can help others. You could even give emotional support or lead this person to Christ in his or her final moments, for it is only God who heals. Sadly, the man died in church. The safety net was not available to him.

As I sat down quietly, I asked myself, are these leads aware of the story of the Good Samaritan in the bible. At that time, the Samaritans were not supposed to help the Jews, let alone even talk to them. Out of his busy schedule, the Samaritan had compassion on a total stranger and helped him.

Jesus said, "'Love the Lord your God with all your heart and with all your soul and with all your strength and with all your mind' and, 'Love your neighbor as yourself.' (Luke 10:27). Furthermore, we love because he first loved us. Whoever claims to love God yet hates a brother or sister is a liar. For whoever does not love their brother and sister, whom they have seen, cannot love God, whom they have not seen. (1 John 4:19-20).

Forgiving

A lead is supposed to forgive, as Christ forgave us our sins by nailing it on the cross, if we believe in Him. When Peter asked Jesus in Matthew 18:21-35, how many times we should forgive someone who has wronged us? Jesus answered we should forgive him seventy times seven times meaning we should forgive anybody who sins against us at all times.

Jesus then told the parable of the unmerciful servant. He likened the kingdom of heaven to a king who wanted to settle accounts with his servant. A man who owed this king 10,000 bags of gold was brought before him. The master ordered that his wife and children be sold to repay the debt. The servant begged the King mercilessly to have pity on him. He cancelled his debt and let him go. That same servant went out and found his fellow servant who owed him 100 silver coins which was lower in value than the cancelled debt he previously owed the king. Instead of showing mercy and forgive the servant as he has been showed mercy. He grabbed him and begun to choke him to pay him back.

He threw the man into prison despite the pleas from him. When the king heard about this incident, he handed him over to the jailers to be tortured until he paid back all what he owed him. Jesus concluded that this is how your heavenly father will treat each of you unless you forgive your brother or sister from your heart.

I was in Church one Sunday, listening to the sermon whilst checking the scriptures on my phone. I was new to this church, I hardly knew anyone around. A boy in his twenties walked briskly into the Church whilst the sermon was going on. He was grinning from ear to ear and I immediately knew, this young man was familiar with the place. The lead stopped the sermon and asked the boy what he was doing in Church. The boy bowed his head in shame and I knew there was a problem.

What was the problem, I begun to pry and listen whether I could get some information from the murmurings which has suddenly turned into a clutter. Apparently, the boy has given some information of the Church to some ex members. I saw nothing wrong with this.

The lead was so furious, shouted at the top of his voice and sacked the boy from Church. I had never seen such attitude from a lead in my whole life. If God forgave you of all your sins, why are you unable to forgive the sins of others too?

In another surprising event as well, I went to a midweek service and the lead announced that he was coming to do something strange and he warned everyone not to talk about it.

Apparently, someone had given information about him to a church member that he never has time for church members. He called the victim; poured olive oil on the church floor lay in it and cursed him. What a sight to behold! That was the straw that broke the camel's back and I realized that I was better off at home. Jesus talks about loving your enemies and praying for them no matter what.

Loving all People

There is neither Jew nor Gentile, neither slave nor free, nor is there male and female, for you are all one in Christ Jesus. (Galatians 3:28). Leads should love all people irrespective of their backgrounds and status in society. There were times, I have been at church and well -dressed congregants were given seats at the front pew and the" have nots" were discriminated. Loving others is putting other people's needs above yours. For the entire law is fulfilled in keeping this one command: "Love your neighbor as yourself." (Galatians 5:14).

Applies wisdom in all situations

In dealing with counseling issues, the lead should apply wisdom in all situations so as not to cause further harm. A lead was counseling a couple that had marital issues. He meddled in their affairs so much that, they resented each other. At the end of it all, the marriage broke down. The book of James tells us, if you lack wisdom ask the Lord. When a lead is presented with such a situation, he should pray about it and ask for the Holy Spirit's guidance. He should put his knowledge and past experiences aside and let the Holy Spirit guide.

Democrat

We are all equal in the sight of God. When we have the opportunity to lead, we should not lord it over people and assume all power and authority. All power and authority belongs to God, we are just hired hands to do the work he uses us to do. We should therefore lead by example, listening to views, comments and suggestions from others as well. However, we should discern the messages of people to know which one God- is given.

Adwoba Addo-Boateng

CHAPTER 7

ALLOW HIM TO STYLE YOUR HAIR

If The Wig Doesn't Fit, Don't Wear It

There are times when we want to do things our own way because we feel that that God's way is not happening the way that we want it or it is keeping too long. However, we should not underplay the sovereignty of God. **Oh, the depth of the riches both of the wisdom and knowledge of God! How unsearchable are His judgments and His ways past finding out! "For who has known the mind of the Lord? Or who has become His counselor?" "Or who has first given to Him and it shall be repaid to him?" For of Him and through Him and to Him are all things, to whom be glory forever. Amen (Romans 11:33-36).**
A young bald woman wanted to go for a job interview at all cost. She had to go! She had stayed at home for ever and this was her chance to earn some money. She was so excited for the D-day. Unfortunately, on the D-day her wig couldn't fit. She tried and tried, her wig couldn't fit and that was the only wig she had. Oh! No! It was such a huge disappointment. Sadly, she couldn't go. The next day, she received the news that the company she was supposed to attend interview at had an unfortunate disaster. The roof caved in and everybody who was there at the time of the interview died. Sometimes, when things are not happening the way we want it, he is preventing something disastrous from happening. He is saving our lives!

Christianity is a lifestyle with Christ. Christianity is not a means of achieving our bucket list and it is not a means of achieving our goal. However, whatever you want you may ask God in prayer and he answers your prayer according to his will (Philippians 4).

When one is a Christian, there is a need to be totally submissive to God for his will to be done. We see things in a different way and we act accordingly but whatever happens to you as a Christian, you keep on holding on to Christ and your faith is built in Christ that whatever happens to you, God is good. He is the one driving, not you. He sees the final picture that you don't see. God is sovereign; allow his sovereignty over your life.

Do It Yourself

You don't know what you have. You don't know what God wants to give you. Don't limit God with your prayers and limit your blessings as well. Even when you pray, open your heart to whatever answer he chooses. God is everywhere you really don't need any spiritual father to lead you. Allow Christ to lead you to your destiny by relying and renewing your hope in the lord.

What we mostly do in these churches can be likened to a young girl in a supermarket who finds a packet of grapes in front of her picks it up and gives it to the cashier and buys it again. Let us learn to pray according to the will of God and according to the dictates of our heart.

Your Spiritual Father Is In Heaven

One will say what about Paul/Timothy's relationship? Paul and Timothy's bond was unique. Timothy was already a disciple of Christ when Paul met him. He was highly spoken off. Now Paul circumcised Timothy and anybody who circumcises someone at that time automatically becomes the father of the circumcised.

Timothy became Paul's adopted son not a spiritual son. Timothy's father was Greek so he could not circumcise him. But then although Paul circumcised Timothy he never lorded his decisions over him. They worked hand in hand and they delivered the decisions reached by the apostles/elders in Jerusalem for the people to obey.

Churches were strengthened in the faith and grew daily in numbers and they both relied on the Holy Spirit. In Acts16:6, when Paul and his companions traveled, they were kept by the Holy Spirit from preaching the word. Paul after the vision, that is hearing from God left for Macedonia.

There's a trend these days in the Churches. I hear a lot of preaching these days "You need a spiritual father for protection. You need covering. Meanwhile that covering can be blown over by any wind. When I really know that the only one who can give you protection is God and we all need covering from God as children of God. He is the overall protector In Matthew 23; 9, Jesus cautioned **"And do not call anyone on earth "father" for you have one Father and he is in heaven**.

What is preventing you from praying to God to ask for protection? There is no barrier in coming to God. In churches these days the spiritual father's influence on God's flock is enormous. Gradually, the spiritual fathers are becoming a substitute for God in people's lives. To the extent that every step you take in your life, you have to tell a spiritual father. Why don't you develop a personal relationship with God and hear from him. Call on God, he will answer you. The Genuine father you could ever have is God and you are greatly assured of His best interest for you. He is the only one you can trust. Most" spiritual fathers" destroy lives.

In marriages, a lot are known to have caused a lot of break ups leading to divorces. Some people listen to their spiritual fathers more than their husbands and it has broken many marriages. Anything that God has designed is anointed and Marriage is an institution designed by God. In 1 Corinthians 11: 13 reads *but I want you to realize that the head of every man is Christ, and the head of the woman is man, and the head of Christ is God.*

When a lady said her vows at the altar, she agreed to have that husband to be her head. So let the Holy Spirit guide you in choosing a husband so that you can make a good decision. Irrespective of whoever you have married, you are supposed to recognize that person as your head even if you feel you made a mistake. The Apostle Paul said in Romans 8:28 And **_we know that all things work together for good to those who love God, to those who have been called according to His purpose._**

A lady in a local church had a very happy marriage; the husband set her up with a small scale business. The business was thriving and then she started using the money to sow seeds because her spiritual father commanded her to do so against her husband's wish. The business finally collapsed and the marriage ended. Note that I am not against seed sowing but God loves a cheerful giver. If the giving is not from your heart, what is the essence? Is your giving to please man or God?

Ephesians 5:22-24 *"Wives, submit yourselves to your own husbands as you do to the Lord. For the husband is the head of the wife as Christ is the head of the church, his body, of which he is the Savior. Now as the church submits to Christ, so also wives should submit to their husbands in everything"*. Some ladies will do everything for their 'spiritual fathers' but will be very disrespectful at home and submission is never in their dictionaries.

Jesus is the Good Shepherd and we are His Sheep

Woe to the shepherds who are destroying and scattering the sheep of my pasture!" declares the LORD. (Jeremiah 23:1). We are all the Lord's people with one leader and that is Christ. Throughout Paul's letter to Timothy, he uses the phrase Christ Jesus that emphasizes the kingly rule of Jesus which served as a reminder to the church that Jesus is the clearest model of authentic leadership.

These leads preach sermons that cause divisions in the Lord's people. Most of the sermons are on how to deal with people who have wronged you. They cause confusion in marriages and in family which causes marriages and families to be dysfunctional. There is always an evil one who causes all the commotion. God gave us earthly families to love and support us through our journey here on earth. If families were not important, the almighty God would not have created it.

Make every effort to keep the **unity** of the Spirit through the bond of peace. There is one body and one Spirit, just as you were called to one hope when you were called; one Lord, one faith, one baptism; one **God** and Father of all, who is over all and through all and in all. (Ephesians 4).

Seeking Ye First the Kingdom Of God.

Seeking ye first the kingdom of God is total submission to God. When we gladly do the work of God, he goes about asking what we want not the other way round. True religion that is faultless is to take care of the poor and needy and to keep oneself unspotted from the world. It is only when we want something that is when we know God, and then we are using God as a means to get to a goal. We should let God be the goal. Our goal is to have an interpersonal relationship with God by communing with him all the time, living according to his word and ultimately remaining in him.

God Is Omnipresent

Leaving Work to Prayer Groups: Anything Is Better Than Nothing

Paul worked in an educational institute; he was a very hard worker who never played with his job. However, he was not that okay with his boss, he felt he was the best person for the position the boss had. He decided to pray for God's intervention to get him a new and better job. He prayed and prayed but to no avail.

He got frustrated and decided to join a church prayer group that meets during working hours. He always took French leaves to join this prayer group to pray. His superiors complained about his attitude towards work, meanwhile he was still showing gross disrespect to his immediate boss.

Everyone at work hated his attitude; a new employee was brought in to help with the work. The new employee was very dutiful and respectful; above all he knew how to serve. A year after, the boss called the new employee (Mark) and asked him whether he would like to take a position in a new company as one of the management team. He was surprised his service has paid off.

When Paul heard about this new position given to Mark by his boss, he was surprised. That was the job he has always been praying for and now it was given to Mark. He did not know that his new job lied in service to his boss. Whatever you do, work at it with all your heart, as working for the Lord, not for human masters, since you know that you will receive an inheritance from the Lord as a reward. It is the Lord Christ you are serving. (Colossians 3:23-24).

God has been downplayed; the omnipresent God suddenly can be found only in Churches. ***"The God who made the world and everything in it is the Lord of heaven and earth and does not live in temples built by human hands" (Acts 17:24)***. If a lead has travelled, you have to wait. Whilst you can go on your knees and pray and the Holy Spirit is there to guide you.

A lady prayed to God for a job and eventually had a job. Although the salary was not what she anticipated, she took it since it could be a stepping stone. She worked diligently and soon won the favor of all her superiors. After a while, a friend introduced her to a prayer group that meets during her office hours. The lead at the prayer group told her to come and pray for God to open a new door for her. She obliged and started taking French leaves to the meeting place.

Her managers got to know about it. She was warned severally but she wanted that new door so badly so she did not pay heed to the warning. After several efforts by her managers to put her on track proved futile, she was eventually sacked. She met one of her managers on her way to the grocery shop. The manager told her how they wanted to give her a new position in a partner firm but her attitude to work was nothing to write home about. She was so sad! The manager went further, that position was actually for you but we had to decline that offer.

Till date she is still unemployed and she has lost interest in the prayer group as well." Everywhere there is God. When we decide to pray at any place, the place becomes spiritually charged with the presence of God. These leads tell their members that the presence of God is only in the church buildings. People have to leave their work places to meet at church where they pray even at the expense of the work. If you believe that it is God who gave you that work so you can take care of your family, you will do it wholeheartedly and efficiently and work for your masters as if you are working for the Lord.

Freedom from Human Rules/ Regulations

Therefore, do not let anyone judge you by what you eat or drink, or with regard to a religious festival a new moon celebration or Sabbath day. These are shadow of the things to come; the reality is, however is found in Christ (Colossians 2:16-17).

Freedom from the Law

The law has been fulfilled when Jesus Christ sacrificed his life for our sake. Paul said in his letter to the Galatians in chapter 2:21 that *"I do not set aside the grace of God, for if righteousness could be gained through the law, Christ died for nothing!"*
For this reason, Christ is the mediator of a new covenant, that those who are called may receive the promised eternal inheritance—now that he has died as a ransom to set them free from the sins committed under the first covenant. (Hebrews 9:15).

The Real Bondage

A young lady brought a perfume to church. The lead asked for perfume to use for something I do not even know. The young lady got up from the pew so hurriedly and gave her perfume to the lead. The lead looked at the name and said "BONDAGE". Apparently the perfume was called "BONDAGE". The lead then said, if you use perfumes with such names then you will really be in "BONDAGE" he stated that as children of God, we should be certain of the type of perfume we buy. The young girl's "BONDAGE perfume was smashed! Hmmm! sarcastically the lead had put that young girl in "BONDAGE by limiting her choices of perfume. When you truly have found Christ, names on perfume mean nothing.

Forbidden Flour

I went to a church and the lead supposedly healed an allegedly HIV Aids patient. He stated categorically, do not eat flour for some time. I was astonished, what has eating flour got to do with healing processes, if the healing is Christ centered, then you truly are healed. The victim was so sad; probably foods made with flour were her favorite food. What happened from there remains another story for another day.

Since you died with Christ to the elemental spiritual forces of this world, why, as though you still belonged to the world, do you submit to its rules: "Do not handle! Do not taste! Do not touch!"? These rules, which have to do with things that are all destined to perish with use, are based on merely human commands and teachings. Such regulations indeed have an appearance of wisdom, with their self-imposed worship, their false humility and their harsh treatment of the body, but they lack any value in restraining sensual indulgence (Colossians 2:20-23)

CHAPTER 8

SAVED WITH AMAZING GRACE (SWAG)

Do you have swag? Is Christ your strength and through him you do all things? Lay hold on your life and let your life be led and influenced by Christ to be actually who you were created to be.
Perfection was not attained through the levitical priesthood that is why Jesus Christ had to come and offer his body as a sacrifice, once and for all. The change in priesthood automatically came with a change in the law (Hebrews 7: 11-12). For the former regulation was set aside because it was weak/ useless for the law made nothing perfect and a better hope is introduced by which we draw near to God (Hebrews 7:18-19). *Jesus is able to save completely those who come to God through him, because he always lives to intercede for them* (Hebrews 7:25).

The Levitical Priesthood: The First Covenant

The old tabernacle
Characteristics:
1. Regulations for worship
2. Earthly Sanctuary

Description of Old Tabernacle
- The first room had a lampstand, table, consecrated bread called holy place.
- Behind the second curtain, there was a room called the most holy place.
- Golden altar of incense
- Gold covered ark of covenant (Ark contained gold jar of manna, Aaron's staff that had budded and the stone tablets of the covenant). Above the ark where the cherubim of glory, overshadowing the atonement cares.

Rituals

The priest entered regularly into the outer room to carry on their ministry. Only the high priest entered the inner room and that only once a year and performed rituals for the atonement of sins.
This is an illustration for the present time, indicating that the gifts and sacrifices being offered were not able to clear the conscience of the worshipper. They are only a matter of food and drink and various ceremonial washings-external regulations, applying until the time of the new order (Hebrews 9:9-10).

The New Covenant Is a Superior Covenant

Hebrews 10: 11-12 says "Day after day every priest stands and performs his religious duties again and again he offers the same sacrifices, which can never take away sins. But when this priest had offered for all time one sacrifice for sins, he sat down at the right hand of God.

Gospel of Truth and Grace

Jesus Christ is the gospel of truth and grace. In the Apostle Paul's letter to the Galatians, he was warning them not to turn to a different gospel other than on Christ. Evidently at that time, people were throwing people into confusion and people were trying to pervert the gospel of Christ. If a lead is not preaching the gospel of truth as laid down by Christ, then the person will be under God's curse. (Colossians 2:8). See to it that no one takes you through hollow and deceptive philosophy, which depends on human tradition and the elemental spiritual forces of this world rather than on Christ.

Servant of Christ

A servant of Christ should not be a people pleaser but should only seek to please God as directed by the Holy Spirit. (Galatians 1:11-13). Servants of Christ should excel in gifts that build up the church. A servant should live a life worthy of the lord and please him in every way: bearing fruit in every good work, growing in the knowledge of God. (Colossians 1:10).

Boasting About Weaknesses

The Apostle Paul in 2 Corinthians 12 said he will rather boast of his weaknesses than boast of his strength. Accordingly, so that no one will think of him, more than what he does or says. Leads are not supposed to be conceited. God kept Paul from being conceited by putting a thorn in his flesh. He pleaded with the Lord, to take it from him and God could have, but he did not. God loves a contrite heart. But he said to Paul, my grace is sufficient for you, in other words, my grace is all you need. His power is made perfect in weakness, when we are weak, then he is strong.

Teachers

Not many of you should become teachers, my fellow believers; because you know that we who teach will be judged more strictly (James 3:1). When a lead does not teach well by relying on the Holy Spirit, he or she distorts the gospel of Christ.

Most leads teach about how the word of God makes one wealthy, which includes the rules to attain wealth. The gospel of Christ does not make one wealthy. Each one has been made in a peculiar way for a specific purpose. It rather leads you to the narrow path so that you can find Christ for your true self to be revealed. *The only way to bear fruits is to remain in him*. (John 15).

True Apostle Defined By the Apostle Paul

The Apostle Paul said his messages should not portray anything different than centered on Christ for Christ rescued us from our sins to rescue us from the present evil age according to the will of God. The authority that God gives is to build people up and not tearing them down (2 Corinthians 13:5).

1 Corinthians 4:9-13 it reads "For it seems to me that God has put us apostles on display at the end of the procession, like those condemned to die in the arena. We have been made a spectacle to the whole universe, to angels as well as to human beings. We are fools for Christ, but you are so wise in Christ! We are weak, but you are strong! You are honored, we are dishonored! To this very hour we go hungry and thirsty, we are in rags, we are brutally treated, and we are homeless. We work hard with our own hands. When we are cursed, we bless; when we are persecuted, we endure it; when we are slandered, we answer kindly. We have become the scum of the earth, the garbage of the world-right up to this moment".

No Divisions in the Church

Churches have been plagued by quarrels and consequently divisions. The Apostle Paul said that churches must be perfectly united in mind and thought. Accordingly, Christ is not divided; Christ is for all in all.

Everybody has a ministry given to him or her by God. Furthermore, everybody and his or her work as well. There are cases, where a lead is supposed to start the church and leave it for another lead to continue. These days every lead wants to start and finish a church for his or her financial gain. Neither the one who plants nor the one who waters is anything, but only God, who makes things grow. The one who plants and the one who waters have one purpose, and they will each be rewarded according to their own labor. For we are co-workers in God's service; you are God's field; God's building (1 Corinthians 3).

Setting Your Minds on Things Above

Setting your mind on earthly things such as money is not Christ like. These leads focus too much on money. Money is used in everything from restoring marriages to buying holy water. You cannot serve God and money .Money is another God that people worship.

Christianity Is a Lifestyle with Christ

In this hustle and bustle of life, everyone is struggling to make ends meet, to cater for his or her family and possibly other people as well. One question that is mind boggling is, should one struggle as a Christian? Jesus told his followers whoever finds his life will lose it, and whoever loses his life for my sake will find it (Matthew 10:39). So then, why are we struggling to find our lives and not losing it for Christ?

I Have Given My Life to Christ

I have given my life to Christ, is a popular saying by many people and we hear it each day. When someone is asked? Are you a Christian? The person replies Oh yes! And most of the time adds, I was born into a Christian home, I never miss church, and I am even in the church choir and so on. Wait a minute, is this what qualifies one as a Christian? Certainly not!

That statement "I have given my life to Christ is a very huge statement" which means you are walking in the footsteps of Christ and he is in charge of your whole life. When we pray the Lord's Prayer as taught by Jesus, we intend to submit to Christ's ruling in our lives that is submitting to the Holy Spirit. Therefore, you live according to the spirit and not according to the flesh. Therefore we are always confident and know that as long as we are at home in the body we are away from the Lord. For we live by faith, not by sight. We are confident, I say, and would prefer to be away from the body and at home with the Lord. (2 Corinthians 5:6-8).

The Apostle Paul mentioned the acts of the flesh in Galatians 5:19-20. The acts of the flesh are obvious: sexual immorality, impurity and debauchery; idolatry and witchcraft; hatred, discord, jealousy, fits of rage, selfish ambition, dissensions, factions and envy; drunkenness, orgies, and the like. I warn you as I did before, that those who live like this will not inherit the kingdom of God. Therefore, the more the flesh is crucified, the closer we get to God, for the flesh kills but the spirit gives life.

Christianity is a Reflection of your Relationship with Others

Many of us are experts in telling God what we want from him. But have we taken a thought to know what God wants from us. God wants us to love him, "If you love me, keep my commands (John 14:15). What is God's greatest commandment? God's greatest commandment is to love the Lord God with all thy heart, soul and mind. But how can we love God that we have not seen. The representation of God is in everyone, not only to the good ones or those who love you or those in your inner circle, but to the poor man on the street, your father or mother who neglected you, your mean boss, the lady who broke your home and your friend who betrayed you.

How can you say you love God when you do not love your brother or sister? You bear grudges with people; you don't want to be friends with your neighbor who reported you to child services for not treating your child well and among others. We are supposed to love this people. God said, if you love those who love you, what credit is that to you?

Even sinners love those who love them. And if you do good to those who are good to you, what credit is that to you? Even Sinners do that. And if you lend to those from whom you expect repayment, what credit is that to you? Even sinners lend to sinners, expecting to be repaid in full. (Luke 6). Experience with God's love even to your enemies and to those who hate you and treat you badly leads to obedience to God's will.

Christianity is not about you, but it is about living selflessly by putting other people's needs above yours. Jesus emphasized in Luke 6:35-36 that "But love your enemies, do good to them, and lend them without expecting to get anything back. Then your reward will be great, and you will be children of the Most High, because he is kind to the ungrateful and wicked. Be merciful, just as your Father is merciful". Therefore we need to let go and let God in our lives.

The Dilemma

A mother was nearing pension and she had nothing to show for all the number of years in service, then she managed to rent a house to use as a preschool. However, her daughter was struggling; she and her husband had hit a low point in their lives. Taking care of the home had become so difficult, like a whirlwind, the landlady was evicting them from where they lived. Here, the mother wanted to use her house for a business entity to survive and on the other hand there was her daughter needing the house to shelter her family. She was adamant at first, not wanting to give the house but eventually she let it out. She did not think of her pension plan anymore but she was thinking of the need of her daughter.

She put her daughter's needs above hers and her daughter lived there with her family. After a while, someone she never fathomed help from bought her a house even bigger than what she gave out. She lost it all for the sake of Christ, she wasn't even thinking about gaining. However, she was able to find her life after losing it all to fulfill a need of someone.

The story of the Good Samaritan that Jesus told, lays emphasis on helping people in need, irrespective of the assumptions, values and belief we may hold. The Jews were not on good terms with the Samaritans, but this man, "deviated" from the norm to fulfill a need.

Then a teacher of the law came to him and said, ***"Teacher, I will follow you wherever you go." Jesus replied, Foxes have dens and birds have nests, but the Son of Man has no place to lay its head. (Matthew 8:20-21).*** Jesus stressed on the need for selflessness in order to follow him and that is the essence of Christianity.

Are you a believer?

Then they asked him, what must we do to do the work that God requires? Jesus answered, the work of God is this: to believe in the one he has sent (John 6:28-29). We believe in the one he has sent if we accept him as the Lord of our lives and make him the ruler of our lives.

A believer is someone who has given his or her life to Christ in totality. He or she has surrendered his or her life to God in submission to the Holy Spirit, because those who are led by the spirit of God are sons of God (Romans 8:14).

If you believe in Christ, then you will obey his instructions by being obedient to his word and that is love The instruction that God gave can be found in John 15:5 "I am the vine; you are the branches, if a man remains in him and I in him, he will bear much fruit; apart from me, you can do nothing. Abiding in the true vine was an instruction that Jesus gave for us as children of God to obey so that we can be fruitful.

One may ask, what does it mean to abide in the true vine, Jesus is the vine and we are the branches. If we abide in the vine that is we take all our nutrients from the vine, we will be fruitful. When we abide in the vine we constantly dwell in his word, we pray without ceasing (1 Thessalonians 5:18) and we wait for his perfect will to be done in whatever situation we may find ourselves in. When we allow God to lead, whilst we follow, we become God's friend and we can ask for whatever we wish and it will be given to us (John 15:7).

God is the Provider of all Needs

Once you are a believer and you are obedient to his word, you also rest in the finished work of Christ, for it is God who works in you to will and to act in order to fulfill his good purpose. (Philippians 2:13). On the contrary, if we do not enter his rest then it is mainly because of disobedience to his word and unbelief. And to whom did God swear that they would never enter his rest if not to those who disobeyed? So we see that they were not able to enter, because of their unbelief (Hebrews 3:18-19).

So in conclusion, if you are not able to abide in the true vine and allow the Holy Spirit to lead you in order to be fruitful and enter his rest, then you are not a believer. You then realize that you struggle to provide for your family instead of allowing the grace to work for you, it does not, therefore depend on man's desire or effort but on God's mercy (Romans 9:16). It doesn't also mean that one should be lazy, when the Holy Spirit is activated in you, you do things that normally you would not do, and it ultimately sparks some urge in you to be productive. Moreover, it does not mean that godliness is a means to financial gain (Timothy 6:6).

When we are godly, our goal is to become content in whatever circumstances we find ourselves in. We continue as Christians to put our hope in God to provide us everything we need and best of all to help us find that path that leads to eternal life. If only for this life we have hope in Christ, we are to be pitied more than all men (1 Corinthians 15:19).
Religion that God our Father accepts as pure and faultless is this: to look after orphans and widows in their distress and to keep oneself from being polluted by the world (James 1:27).

Everyone Is Uniquely Created

Everyone and the way he or she is born and the destiny he or she has. Christianity does not make one rich. Money is a gift which has been given to some people and not all people. In Matthew 19:12, Jesus made mention of the fact that people are born eunuchs, so we can draw the conclusion that everyone and the way he or she is born. However, these leads tell members they have to be rich by all means possible meanwhile that is not the case. In addition, when you find Christ, whatever situation you are in or however you are born, you become content. For godliness with contentment is great gain. Paul said I have learnt to be content whatever the circumstances (Philippians 4).

A Different Path: Life in the Spirit

Those who are led by the spirit are called children of God. When God takes you off a path that you are on and leads you on a different path. We at times wonder, and normally we do not like it. It just looks different, sometimes, it is uncomfortable. As Christians we need to trust the path and follow the lead that is Jesus to lead out in any situation we may be in. Normally, it leads us to a place we never imagined we could be. ***Now to him who is able to do immeasurably more than all we ask or imagine, according to his power that is at work within us.*** (Ephesians 3:20) Sometimes, when God gives us instructions, we find it difficult to follow those instructions, owing to the fact that we are so used to doing things our own way. Accordingly, that may also be the norm. Why deviate from the norm? When God told me to write books, it was a very difficult time of my life. My job contract had just ended. We could hardly fend for ourselves from my husband's salary.

Things were indeed tough. I put everything away and concentrated on God's work. It was a tough decision. My family was against it, they thought I had lost it. The distractions were many, for some strange reason, but I looked up to only Christ. But I still concentrated on God. When everything seems hopeless and going nowhere, you just have to trust the process.

That does not mean there will not be temptations, ***No temptation has overtaken you except what is common to mankind. And God is faithful; he will not let you be tempted beyond what you can bear. But when you are tempted, he will also provide a way out so that you can endure it.*** (1 Corinthians

10;13) There were times, I was not able to write due to distractions in the world, but I had to lose it all for Christ. *For whoever wants to save their life will lose it, but whoever loses their life for me will find it. What good will it is for someone to gain the whole world, yet forfeit their soul? Or what can anyone give in exchange for their soul?* (Matthew 16:25-26)).

Furthermore I was seeking ye first the kingdom of God and His righteousness and all other things would be added to it (Matthew 6:33). Furthermore, I was abiding in the Lord in order to be fruitful. Before one has to be fruitful he or she has to remain in Christ. Moreover, when you remain in Christ, he prunes you so that you will be more fruitful. (John 15). It also built my faith and trust to the extent that God became my all dependency. I was relying on him for everything. I had become God's friend. Jesus said I am the vine; you are the branches. *If you remain in me and I in you, you will bear much fruit; apart from me you can do nothing.* (John 15:5) And if you ask anything according to his will he hears you. *Greater love has no one than this: to lay down one's life for one's friends* (John 15:13).

My interpersonal relationship with God had grown so much to the extent that I allowed him to handle everything concerning me and he did such an excellent job. Things that I was not even expecting were given to me without stress. At times, I would not even pray for it and it will be given to me. There are a lot of good things in store for you if you let go of yourself and trust the one at the wheel.

Topsy Turvy

Ohemaa lived in an affluent neighborhood, she had it all. She was a writer and a student, when she dropped her kids off at a very prestigious school every morning, she will quickly go to school and at her leisure time, she will write her books. This was her routine and everything was going on well. On the other hand, her husband worked in a reputable organization where he headed the marketing division.

Like a whirlwind, everything started falling apart, her husband lost his job, they could no longer afford that school for their kids, they could not pay their rent and they were served with an eviction notice. All of a sudden their lives changed, they had no place to go to. Ohemaa prayed to God for a solution to their predicament. God answered her prayer. Her mum offered her a cottage on a farm house where they could live in until they get their acts organized. She has never lived in such a house, it was way too small and archaic. Besides, she has lived in a city all her life, how could she cope with life in the suburbs.

She started seeking her own solutions but it was to no avail. She definitely had no choice and she said to herself, may be that is where God wanted me to live. Although adamant from the beginning, she began to trust the process of letting God reign. She went there with her family; her husband found another job and hope was revived. Since the neighborhood was deprived, she set up a not for profit organization to affect lives. She started by donating items to people living in extreme poverty and it metamorphosed into a very big organization with about 20, 000 workers across the globe.

God redirected her path into her destiny. Initially, she felt it was a demotion but it was a promotion. (Humble yourselves and God will lift you up in due time). There may be a lot of dust on the gold, but trusting God through the process will help you find the gold. She lived one day at a time and God took care of the rest.

On another note, a lady's husband got transferred to the country side and of course the whole family had to move along. She homeschooled her kids and that was the beginning of a great school. She is now living a fulfilled life. There are so many uncertainties in life, one thing that is certain is that God can set you free and he always finds a way out through all situations, if we allow him.

Letting Go

Sika was a nagging wife, her nights with her husband where characterized by quarrels, fights and arguments. In fact they were not happy in the marriage; they felt they had married the wrong partner. Things took a different turn when Sika decided to make God the center of her life. The bible talks of submission in marriage. She begun to adhere to the words of the bible, ***for the wisdom of this world is foolishness in God's sight. As it is written: "He catches the wise in their craftiness";*** (1 Corinthians 3:19).

She let everything go and allowed Jesus to take the wheel. God changed her heart completely; she was reverted to her true self. She was such a sweet and loving lady every man will dream off. Her husband also changed as the wife was submitting to him, he loved his wife so profoundly. That is what the gospel of Christ does, when your will is in his will, he makes all things beautiful.

Growing Up Isn't Fun

When we want to see Jesus, we should behave like children, put our worldly knowledge away and follow his path. I always want to be a child of God, not a man of God where I will be nursed with breast milk. Like new born babies, crave spiritual milk, so that by it you may grow up in your salvation (1 Peter 2:2). Until one comes to God with a childlike mind, it is difficult to find him and be in him. Jesus said "suffer the little children to come to me, for theirs is the kingdom of heaven. (The kingdom of heaven belongs to such as these).

A baby believes that his or her mum is all knowing, and therefore has his or her full trust in her. In a similar way, a child is fully dependent on the mum for survival; they are helpless without their mum (guardian) until we lose our guards and become fully dependent on him so that he can be our all sufficiency we are not there yet.

In all your ways, acknowledge him and he will direct your paths.

Jesus said in Matthew 19:14 that let the little children come to me, and do not hinder them, for the kingdom of heaven belong to such as these. God loves the humble; every leader should be like a child before God, for God to work through him or her for he causes us to will and to do when we are in him.

The Good Seed

The word of God is the good seed that will enable us to be fruitful. When a good seed does not get good soil to grow in, although the seed may be good, it may not grow well. The soil should be clear and good enough to enable the seed grow to its maximum potential.

The Parable of the sower told by Jesus, tells us of how our hearts that is the soil is the only determinant of whether a good seed will grow to its maximum potential. The word of God is always true but most at times; our hearts are not clear and opened to receive the word of God. Accordingly, we often do not understand it owing to how dirty our hearts are.

According to Jesus, the seed that fell on the way side and the birds took away signifies the fact that we always hear the word of God but our hearts are not receptive to it, then the devil takes it away. The seed that fell on the rocky ground is the one who hears the word of God, receives it with joy and it is not able to impact their lives. The seed that fell among thorns relates to someone who hears the word of God but the worries of life and the deceitfulness of wealth does not make the word of God grow well in his or her life. (Matthew 13).

When we are constantly in the flesh then we are away from the Lord. We need to crucify the flesh so that we can be close to God, by letting ourselves go and heeding to the spirit. The word of God is true at all times; we should check our soil that is our heart if we are not productive.

God Loves A Cheerful Giver

When we give to the Lord, we must give with our hearts. Leads should not force or trick people to give when it is not their will. They should allow everyone who wants to give to give freely. The widow who gave the two coins gave the greatest according to Jesus, even though people gave out more money. She gave out all she had willingly to help the church.
When we give, we should not let the left hand know what the right hand is doing. We should give in secret so that we our heavenly father who sees what is given in secret will reward one openly.

Jesus at the Wheel

We should allow Jesus to take the wheel and drive us to our destination. When Jesus takes the wheel, it does not mean there will not be bumps on the road, there may be some bumpy rides and smooth rides but when Jesus is at the wheel even if it is a bumpy ride he is at the wheel, he will drive you out of that bump. There may be storms, but with Jesus at the wheel you will smile at the storm. When there is a ditch, he steers you away from falling into a ditch maybe into a bump and takes you out of there in due time. Sometimes, there is a traffic light pole on the road, the red has lighted and you need to stop, if you do not pay heed to this instruction you will crush. After a while, the green light will be on, and then you can proceed.

There was a time in my life, when I was faced with so many difficulties. We were expecting a check that was not forthcoming. We relied so much on this check that it was such a huge disappointment to us that it had delayed. All our plans were halted, we were going to use the check to pay rent, school fees, feed the home and all other needs and wants. We thought money was going to solve our problems but it let us down completely. All of a sudden, our lives took a different turn to the extent that we could not afford meals for the children.

Our lives were stopped, literally. Surprisingly, there was no one to even borrow money from. It was hard! There was so much pain in my heart, but quickly I reminded myself that God is turning the wheel to another path that he has created for me. There is therefore the need to stop or slow down before negotiating that bend. I forgot about the money and told God to take control of the situation. After suffering for a while, his glory was revealed and this time I understood that money was not the solver but God was. We had a free house and somehow the kids went to school without that money we were thinking could solve the problem. You indeed cannot serve God and money

Ministers of the New Covenant

The ministry through the spirit that is Christ is greater than the ministry of the letter that is the covenant under Moses. Moses' covenant although fading was glorious anytime the letter was read, how much glorious will Christ ministry be since it brings about righteousness. When Moses is read, a veil covers their hearts (face) and it is only in Christ that it is taken away. The old has been made obsolete and what is obsolete will soon pass away. When our faces are unveiled through Christ we are able to see clearly because the eye is the light of our body. When our eye is able to see clearly our whole body is full of light. Then we are being transformed to God's image with ever increasing glory (2 Corinthians 3).

In Jesus, There Is Power

When Peter and John were going up to the temple, they met a lame man on the way. He was crippled from birth. The lame man asked Peter and John to give him alms, but Peter and John said; we have something greater than money to give you. In the name of Jesus Christ of Nazareth, walk. Immediately, he received his miracle and begun walking and praising God (Acts 3).

A real lead of a Church should be a shepherd of God's flock that is under your care not pursuing dishonest gain from them. By taking money from people when you are not supposed to and most importantly you should be eager to serve all manner of people. At the end of it all God will glorify you in His own time. You should learn to clothe yourself with humility. God opposes the proud and shows favor to the humble. God is the only one who can lift you up, stand firm in faith after long suffering, he will restore you.

There's no easy way out. It is just to make you stronger. Therefore we do not lose heart. Though outwardly we are wasting away, yet inwardly we are being renewed day by day. (2 Corinthians 4:16) Let us rely on the true grace of God which is available to all when you receive Christ.

A real pastor is to lead you to Christ and give godly counseling where need be not to create fear and panic and of course wealth from you. All the spiritual gifts given to leads work together in unity, In 1 Thessalonians 5:21. You test all things by prayer and hold fast to what is good. The Holy Spirit is free and available to all and there to guide us.

Let Jesus Christ be your only lead. Activate your holy spirit and let it be your guide in this journey. When the disciples started fellowshipping together, they needed a new member to replace Judas, they prayed together for a leader and God chose Matthias. They were all filled with the Holy Spirit and spoke the word of God boldly without fear.

However as humans as they were they had their own disagreements but the goal to preach Christ was attained because Christ was the focus not them. Paul said " However, I consider my life worth nothing to me; my only aim is to finish the race and complete the task the Lord Jesus has given me—the task of testifying to the good news of God's grace" (Acts 20:24).

Pride goes before a fall

Every leader's goal is to focus on Christ to make an impact in people's life to the glory of God in order to magnify him. However, these days, most leads aim is to chase after social status and recognition from people. For, as I have often told you before and now tell you again even with tears, many live as enemies of the cross of Christ. Their destiny is destruction, their god is their stomach, and their glory is in their shame. Their mind is set on earthly things (Philippians 3:18-19).

Furthermore, most leads compare their ministry to others and it breeds unhealthy competition forgetting that everyone has a distinct gift that God has deposited in him or her. For instance, Ministry A is organizing a church program and church attendance is low. He or she begins to compare his or her ministry to Ministry B. He or she then forces his church members to do things that they normally will not do to outperform the other Ministry.

Christianity is never forcing people to do things out of their own will but rather freedom of worship in Christ Jesus. It is a wrong misconception that people have that the larger your congregation or building, the greater your ministry. Your ministry is greater when you have humbled yourself under God's hands to serve others and he has used you to impact lives. Christ is our role model, we are supposed to imitate Christ and follow in his exemplary life.

Moreover, some leads also feel that they should never be criticized even when they are doing something wrong. Meanwhile some criticism are constructive that makes you a better person. Anytime, someone tries to give a word of advice they become defensive and do not open their hearts to receive the message. God always give us messages through people. It is up to us to pray for discernment.

I once knew a lead who had a problem with his wife, he always beat his wife at the least provocation and when an elderly man tried to advise him on that, he begun to justify the beating of his wife. No beating is justified no matter the wrong the person has done, it is never Christ like.

Some leads also boast whilst preaching and the essence of the message is on how rich they are and not on Christ. Christianity is never a means to get rich, but a means to fulfillment in Christ. They begin to depend on the riches they have acquired instead of depending on the Holy Spirit and trusting God in all circumstances. A lead should be open and transparent in all his or her ways most importantly in his or her weakness to his congregation. Just that one must be careful that what he or she is sharing is for the uplifting of others in a similar situation that God really is.

Furthermore, most leads use the dictatorship rule in leading the church. They do not embrace other views and opinions from others. They also want to be served instead of rather serving others. Exhibiting a compassionate heart in serving those in need is a far cry from them. They also do not empower others to lead, they want to be in control and whatever they say is final and it cannot be challenged.

When we walk into a salon to get our hair done, we meet the hair dresser with great customer care skills. We eventually give him or her, the permission to make our hair into whatever style we choose. Relying on the fact that he or she is an expert in the field, we trust him or her so much that we relax and wait for the final product of our hair. In actual fact, the pastors and leads are apprentices or helping hands, but the real hair dresser is Christ. Christ is the only one who can dress our hair into whatever he chooses. Let us give Christ the chance to make our hair for us in ways unimaginable. Pastors and leads are hired hands; they are not the real shepherd who takes care of the sheep.

The Lord Is My Shepherd (Psalm 23)

As good a shepherd as the Lord is, he cares for his sheep no matter what. He died on the cross to save his sheep. I am the good shepherd. The good shepherd gives his life for the sheep (John 10:11). The sheep is totally reliant on the Shepherd although prone to wander, to receive utmost care from the sheep. (John 10:27). He leads us in his way all we have to do is to be his sheep and submit to his will.

We cannot see God as the Shepherd if we don't see ourselves us his sheep. A sheep is totally submissive to his Shepherd, owing to the fact that the Shepherd leads the way for the Sheep to follow.

The Sheep trusts that it is the best way. The more a sheep needs its shepherd, the more the Shepherd provides for his sheep. If a sheep feels that he feed himself on his own, he wanders and drifts away from the Shepherd.

"I shall not want" in Psalm 23 signifies one being fulfilled in Christ. Even when we want something and we do not get, the peace that he promises us overrides our wants. It does not mean that we do not lack but even in the lack God's love is sufficient for us manifested by the grace which he bestows on us. His grace is available to all when you have humbled yourself enough to be his sheep by believing in him. His grace is sufficient for us (Scripture). "Yea though I walk in the valley of the shadow of death" Even when all is bleak, dark I still remain in his love. Who shall separate us from the love of Christ? Shall tribulation, or distress, or persecution, or famine, or nakedness, or peril, or sword? (Romans 8:35).

When God is leading us we don't care even if we are in a dark point. God is still providing and protecting us in the dark moments. No temptation has overtaken you except what is common to man; but God is faithful, who will not allow you to be tempted beyond what we are able, but with the temptation will also make a way out for escape, that you may be able to bear it (1 Corinthians 10:13). Even though we are broken, in despair, God is still enough for us.
"He makes us lie down in green pastures" God allows us to rest so that he can work. He fights battles for us because he is a mighty warrior.

"He restores my soul" Even when I am weak, then he is strong (Christ's power will rest on me). When I am tired, he renews my strength. And do not be conformed to this world, but be transformed by the renewing of your mind, that you may prove what is that good and acceptable and perfect will of God (Romans 12).

"In the presence of my enemies thou anoint my head with oil" Christ is the anointed one. When you have Christ, you can partake of the Lord's goodness and mercy and with the Holy Spirit's guidance you move away from the sin that entangles and you are in his presence every day and God is magnified. Let us continue to have faith in Christ, and drive one another on towards love and good deeds, not giving up meeting each other but encouraging one another in the Lord (Hebrews 10)

Adwoba Addo-Boateng

It Is Not Just A Haircut

Adwoba Addo-Boateng

www.ingramcontent.com/pod-product-compliance
Lightning Source LLC
Chambersburg PA
CBHW052151110526
44591CB00012B/1944